The Gala Planner & Record-Keeper

Capital Books Inc.
P.O. Box 605
Herndon, Virginia 20172-0605

ISBN 1-892123-53-3   (alk. paper)

Library of Congress Cataloging-in-Publication Data

Coons, Patricia.
    The gala planner & record-keeper for professionals, volunteers, chair persons & committee members / Patti Coons.
        p.   cm.
    ISBN 1-892123-53-3
        1. Special events—Planning—Handbooks, manuals, etc.   2. Special events—Management—Handbooks, manuals, etc. I. Title: Gala planner and record-keeper for professionals, volunteers, chair persons & committee members. II. Title.

GT3405.C64   2001
394.2′068—dc21

                                                            2001025487

Designed by Pen & Palette Unlimited

Printed in the United States of America on acid-free paper that meets the American National Standards Institute Z39-48 Standard.

First Edition

10 9 8 7 6 5 4 3 2 1

Contents

Introduction

Congratulations on your appointment as chair of your organization's big charity event! Whether you are new to the game or an experienced professional, this handy planning workbook and record-keeper will make your job easier. Start out by reading my companion book, *Gala! The Special Event Planner for Professsionals and Volunteers*, which provides a comprehensive overview of how to put together a successful fund raiser or charity event, then use this planner to record the details. It, too, provides details and tips you and other chair people on your team need, to organize your event month-by-month—from planning to cleanup, including press releases, public-service announcements, media contact information, and guest-list pages. You'll also find samples of thank-you notes, invitations, and report forms.

The Gala Planner & Record-Keeper also provides space for you and each of your subcommittee chairs to record notes and monitor completion of each responsibility through the months ahead. Keep those vital records and samples in these pages, so you'll have a complete guide for next year's event team. It will make next year's event much easier to produce.

- Non-controversial.
- Able to work with many personalities.
- Able to quash his or her own ego for the good of the event.
- Able to delegate.
- Willing to shoulder the responsibility when someone doesn't follow through.
- Willing to ask for help—both for information and advice.
- Receptive to ideas from others.

Selecting the Event and the Cause

What Kind of Event?

When you begin to consider what kind of a special or charity event your team will put on, keep these things in mind:

- You want to raise as much money as possible for your chosen charity.
- You want to involve as many people as possible.
- You want to attract as much media coverage as possible.

Your responsibility is to create and maintain community interest in your cause. In doing so, your organization's visibility and credibility will rise, and you'll attract the kind of donations and guests you need to make the event a financial success.

From the very start, involve the press in your event and fund-raising endeavors. Media involvement is vital, because the press has the power to influence the triumph of your project. Be sure to include all the press—magazines, AM and FM radio, daily and weekly newspapers, and broadcast and cable television. Every event benefits from frequent mention in the press. Every event gains stature in the public's mind when the press covers it.

What Cause?

Many types of organizations raise money. Auxiliaries or supporters for nonprofit organizations, such as libraries, PTAs, hospital auxiliaries, museum guilds, and Friends of the Zoo raise money regularly. Companies, large and small, often support charities as a way of giving back to the community. Philanthropic groups and civic organizations fund causes they believe in.

Pick a cause that fits the characteristics and goals of your organization and the community you hope to involve. If your group is made up of teenagers, for example, a fund-raising effort focused on buying books for a homeless shelter may galvanize their enthusiasm. If your business is in a historic building, support the local historic preservation society with your event. If your organization is for women, consider charities that benefit women and families. The charity you select should always interest your core committee and the members of your larger group; otherwise, they will not be enthusiastic about the project, and their enthusiasm is crucial in the months ahead. When your committee meets, its members will know it is to work for a cause you all believe in.

Matching the Event to the Cause

Many nonprofit organizations must raise funds to support themselves. In recent years, the women's committee of the National Symphony Orchestra in Washington, D.C., for example, has donated the proceeds from its annual Show House to the orchestra operating budget, an increasingly valuable contribution in a town with few large corporations to support the arts. Public radio and television stations, despite federal appropriations, must conduct fund-raising campaigns regularly to make their budgets. PTAs and booster clubs are other examples of organizations that have clearly defined missions. These organizations each have a cause. They need to choose the kind of event that will highlight their mission, but even more importantly, generate the funds they need to survive.

If your cause is not well known, it may be your first job to define your cause and who it benefits. An event can do that for you.

With a charity selected, you must decide what type of event you want: a one-shot fund raiser or several coordinated events over an extended period of time to reach an overall goal. The possibilities are endless. The only limit is your imagination.

Here is a short list of the kinds of events you might hold:

- **Coffee**—A relatively simple way to entertain a large group of prospective voters for a political candidate with coffee and light refreshments in someone's home, a hotel restaurant, or meeting room. A series of coffees can lead up to the main event or be used to educate potential supporters.

- **Reception**—A more elaborate way to entertain prospective donors or contributors and to introduce representatives for a cause or a candidate, particularly a celebrity who supports the cause. Receptions are usually held in a large public room, club, or sizable private home. Drinks and hors d'oeuvres are served as refreshments.

- **Luncheon**—A sit-down or buffet occasion is appropriate as an annual fund-raising event, because it offers an elegant lunch and accompanying entertainment, such as a speaker or a fashion show.

- **Dinner or formal gala**—Often a much more formal event, which, because it is perceived as something special (elegant menu, creative theme, elaborate flowers and decorations, high-powered speakers and entertainment, often dancing and evening dress), can command a high price-per-person contribution.

- **Afternoon tea**—An increasingly popular and elegant way to entertain people and raise funds for a cause without the elaborate food and expense of a luncheon or dinner.

- **Art show or auction**—A labor-intensive but effective event for raising large amounts of money for a cause. An energetic and capable committee is necessary to amass and sell a wide range of art or contributed goods in one or many categories. Featuring the art of one well-known artist also can be highly lucrative for your charity.
- **Cocktail lecture**—Less work, because only one entertainment (the lecture) is offered. A good event for reaching a large group of people interested in your cause. If an author is speaking, you can also sell his or her book for a portion of the proceeds.
- **Craft workshop, how-to seminar**—Whether flower arranging, financial planning, or bead stringing, a how-to program is an excellent community or club event, particularly if it supports an association of artists or craftspeople or a cultural group.
- **Community garage sale**—An effective moneymaker if you have a large local group interested in one cause and willing to donate items, time, and the proceeds.
- **Sports event**—From a celebrity exhibition or tournament to a Little League championship, a sports event is an entertaining way to raise funds for a cause.
- **Home or garden tour**—A great way to feature a community cause by putting it on display. Requires a large number of volunteers to open their homes or gardens and many more to act as hosts and hostesses.
- **Christmas-decorations competition or holiday greens sale**—A seasonal approach to fund-raising allows the holiday spirit to stimulate contributions.
- **Marathon event** (walk-a-thon, swim-a-thon, dance-a-thon, etc.)—From an official 26-mile, 385-yard marathon to a local walk-a-thon for the community food bank, a marathon event requires sponsors for the event itself and many volunteers, including participants who

- **Cleanup Chair**—Select an operations-minded person who has patience and who dutifully follows up, regardless of the hour.

Calendar

Establishing Your Event Calendar

When you plan a publicity campaign that will encourage people to take action throughout the year, whether to donate to the United Way or become a member of a museum guild, you will use a twelve-month calendar. Generally, one large event will form the keystone of your campaign, and you will plan for that event on a nine-month schedule.

In addition, you may need to plan some smaller satellite events throughout the year to spark enthusiasm, increase awareness and membership, and generate action and contributions in the community. The large event and the smaller ones must be carefully coordinated, so your organization is not overtaxed and each event can shine. As soon as your wrap-up meeting is done for the entire year, you'll start planning for the next year.

Many major events also take a year to plan. For either a yearlong campaign or a major event, complete the groundwork listed in the calendar for Months One and Two at least six months before the event.

Many events can be pulled off with flair, starting only a few months ahead of time. You may even put on an event Fast!—within a few weeks. Whether you plan to do a yearlong campaign, a mid-size event, or a Fast! event, you must follow some basic steps. The following calendar contains the fundamental checkpoints for almost any event, although the months may have to be condensed to fit your timetable. The chair for each task is indicated in parentheses.

Calendar Checklist for a Yearlong Campaign or Major Event

Month One

(Seven to ten months before major event)
Overall Goals:

- Organize.

- Gather information and contacts.

- Customize this calendar to your specific needs.

❑ Determine what kind of event you would like to hold, such as a luncheon, reception, seminar, cocktail lecture, formal or informal dinner, or a variety of separate events as part of a campaign. (Event Chair)

❑ Set goals for your event. (Event Chair)

❑ Determine timeline needed to accomplish each event. (Event Chair)

❑ Recruit your event team. (Event Chair)

❑ Solicit proposals from caterers and other vendors. (Food and Drink Chair)

❑ Determine your target audience and create a mailing list. (Mailing List Chair)

❑ Contact the headquarters of your charity, if one exists, to find out what material they can provide. Ask to use the charity's mailing list and share prior fund raiser efforts. (Charity Chair)

❑ Ask that the charity's executive director or a representative attend all your event-team meetings. (Charity Chair)

❑ Reserve a site. (Arrangements Chair)

❑ Gather the names, addresses, phone and fax numbers, and e-mail or Web site addresses of helpful local business and community leaders. (Donations Chair)

❑ Assemble a media contact list. Identify media you wish to target: magazines, newspapers, radio, and TV. Check carefully for correct addresses and appropriate contacts. (Public Relations Chair)

❑ Establish a Web site. Appoint a knowledgeable person to be in charge of it and keep the site updated. (Public Relations Chair)

Month Two

(At least six months before major event)
In general:

- Form your event team and assign duties.
- Become well informed about the charity or institution you are supporting.
- Expand contacts.
- Gather ideas for future or subsidiary events.

❑ Refine mailing and invitation lists. (Mailing List Chair)

❑ Schedule and plan any seminars you wish to do as part of the fund-raising campaign or event publicity. (Donations Chair)

❑ Contact local, state, or national organizations to set up announcements or public-speaking engagements for presentations about the charity or event you're sponsoring. (Public Relations Chair)

❑ Prepare all presentation material that you will give to the boards of groups you approach for support. (Public Relations Chair)

❑ If you are fund-raising for a charity, contact the charity's central office (which may be at the national, state, or city level) to obtain brochures, slides shows, videos, or other promotional material. (Charity Chair)

❑ Prepare and send press releases and press kits announcing the event or fund raiser. Include information about both your organization and the projects or program you're supporting. (Public Relations Chair)

❑ Update Web site. (Public Relations Chair)

Month Three

(Five months before major event)
In general:

- Make sure the event team committees are on track.

❑ Refine mailing list. (Mailing List Chair)

❑ Write and design the invitation. Be sure to include all necessary information and clear directions. (Invitation Chair)

❑ Offer to speak to local organizations such as the Rotary Club, hospital auxiliary, museum guilds, neighborhood associations, special-interest clubs, and schools. Ask them to support your cause, either financially or with contributions of time or resources. (Donations Chair)

❑ Sponsor seminars of interest to the public or to civic or hobby associations, for example, Junior League and garden clubs. (Donations Chair)

❑ Send out press releases before and after you have a speaking engagement or seminar. Include a photo from the speaking engagement with your "after" release. (Public Relations Chair)

❑ Follow up your contacts network with information and opportunities for participation. (Donations Chair)

❑ Contact local companies for contributions and sponsorships. (Donations Chair)

❏ Make physical arrangements for the event, such as firming up the location, spokesperson, food, entertainment, and audiovisual needs. (Arrangements Chair)

❏ Be certain to have adequate parking. Where space is limited, you may want to offer valet parking. (Arrangements Chair)

❏ Determine whether cellular telephones and pagers work at indoor event sites, especially if doctors, lawyers, or other professional people are attending. If the site is wireless unfriendly, make certain telephones are readily accessible. (Arrangements Chair)

❏ Continue contacting active members of the community, interest groups, media, city officials, key community leaders. (Donations Chair)

Month Four

(Four months before major event)
In general:

- Make sure your event team is getting its work done.

❏ Conduct public speaking engagements and seminars. (Donations Chair)

❏ Make sure key officials and active members of the community know about your event. (Public Relations Chair)

❏ Order invitations. Proof invitations carefully! Have several proofreaders; each should initial the proof. (Invitation Chair)

❏ Keep media contacts well informed. Give them detailed information about the date, time, and place. (Public Relations Chair)

❏ Continue to send out press releases before and after speaking engagements, including a photo of the speaking engagement with the "after" release. (Public Relations Chair)

❏ Select and order souvenirs. (Arrangements Chair)

Month Five

(Three months before major event)
In general:

- Follow up with your event team.

❑ Send advance invitations to sponsors and underwriters. (Invitation Chair)

❑ Send invitations to prominent people. (Invitation Chair)

❑ Continue speaking to special interest groups. (Donations Chair)

❑ If you have a charity spokesperson, follow up to make sure your event is on his or her schedule and that the logistics are worked out. (Public Relations Chair)

❑ Continue networking with officials and community business leaders. (Public Relations Chair)

❑ Send the appropriate media a press release about the event team itself. Include a photo of the event team members. (Public Relations Chair)

❑ Continue to send out press releases before and after public speaking engagements. (Public Relations Chair)

❑ Update Web site. (Public Relations Chair)

❑ Follow up with arrangements for catering, rentals, and other physical details. (Arrangements Chair)

❑ Finalize invitation and mailing list. (Invitation Chair)

Month Six

(Two months before the event)
In general:

- Make sure event team is meeting deadlines.

❑ Continue public speaking engagements. (Event Chair, Donations Chair)

☐ Prepare to mail invitations four to six weeks before your event, if it is a massive one. Otherwise, wait until three or four weeks in advance. (Invitation Chair)

☐ Schedule a gathering of committee members to hand-address invitations. (Invitation Chair)

☐ Have committee members write personal notes to include with or on the invitation. (Invitation Chair)

☐ Immediately follow up on the invitations sent to key invitees to ask for their commitment to attend your event. (Invitation Chair)

☐ Follow up event arrangements. (Arrangements Chair)

☐ Meet, perhaps over lunch, with key officials or community business leaders to discuss charity and stimulate more interest and involvement. (Public Relations Chair)

☐ Target business and community organizations, key city officials, and interest groups to ask for donations. (Donations Chair)

☐ Send a press release about the event accompanied by a photo of key people in your organization with the endorsing celebrity, spokesperson, or charity sponsor. (Public Relations Chair)

☐ Decide when and how your event will conclude. (Arrangements Chair)

Month Seven

(One month before the event)
In general:

• Keep checking up with the event team and go through the final preparation checklist.

☐ Determine who will be in the receiving line. (Event Chair)

❏ Take a key official or community business leader to lunch to discuss your event and stimulate more interest and involvement. (Event Chair)

❏ Confirm speaker and entertainment. Arrange for a back-up speaker in case an emergency prevents your first choice from appearing. (Entertainment Chair or Arrangements Chair)

❏ Have the hotel food service or caterer prepare and present a trial dinner for a small number of committee numbers. (Food and Drink Chair)

❏ As invitations are mailed and responses received, follow up with phone calls. By calling, you make sure the invitation was received and all the information about the event is clear. (Invitation Chair)

❏ Prepare a realistic agenda/schedule for speakers, participants, and entertainment with specific time limits, and confirm with participants. (Arrangements Chair)

❏ Prepare a printed program, if appropriate. (Program Chair)

❏ If you are conducting a yearlong campaign, hold a seminar the public will want to attend. (Event Chair)

❏ Keep in touch with business and community organizations, interest groups, and key city officials. (Event Chair and Donations Chair)

❏ Send out press releases and public service announcements about the event, stating location and event goals. (Public Relations Chair)

❏ Update Web site. (Public Relations Chair)

❏ Post signs in public places announcing the event, if appropriate. (Public Relations Chair)

❏ Review assignments with committee for day of the event. (Event Chair)

❑ Reserve mobile phones or intercom for committee members to keep in touch with each other during the event, if logistics warrant it. (Arrangements Chair)

❑ Be prepared for the unexpected, for example, bad weather, speaker cancellation, rain date, tent. (Arrangements Chair)

❑ Plan for a medical professional, such as a company nurse, to be on hand for emergencies during the event. (Arrangements Chair)

❑ Arrange transportation for dignitaries and guest speakers who need it. (Arrangements Chair)

One week before the event

❑ Send a final press release to media you are targeting. Include new noteworthy information, such as celebrities or dignitaries expected to attend. (Public Relations Chair)

❑ Make follow-up calls to media five days before the event. Call until you have definite answers. (Public Relations Chair)

❑ Confirm refreshments, audio equipment, seating, rest rooms, first aid, photographer, supplies, flowers, décor, entertainment, and so forth. (Arrangements Chair)

❑ Review and update R.s.v.p. list daily. (Invitation Chair)

❑ Keep in daily contact with the caterer, for changes in the number of expected guests. Caterers will require you to give a guarantee by a specific date. After that date, numbers can only go up. (Food and Drink Chair)

❑ Finalize the program and have it printed. (Program Chair)

❑ Prepare a step-by-step agenda for the big day. Include *all* pertinent information on this staging guide. (Program Chair)

❑ Conduct a dress rehearsal of the event with core committee members from start to finish. If that is not possible, at least check the sound system. (Arrangements Chair)

❏ If possible, have the keynote speaker rehearse. If this is not feasible, make sure he or she knows what to do from the moment of arrival through departure. (Arrangements Chair)

❏ Confirm that your staging guide is realistic: Double-check times and set time limits for speakers, entertainment, participants, and the core committee. (Arrangements Chair)

Day of the event

❏ Be organized so you can start on time. (Event Chair)

❏ Follow the confirmed staging guide. (Event Chair)

❏ Allow for extra time, because something will always go wrong. (Arrangements Chair)

❏ Provide transportation for dignitaries and guest speakers who need it. (Arrangements Chair)

❏ Distribute confirmed agenda to keynote speakers, participants, and core committee. Make sure they know what to do. (Arrangements Chair)

❏ Set up media registration table with press kits. (Public Relations Chair)

❏ Display table assignments at the entry. (Arrangements Chair)

❏ Be sure greeters or ushers are in place. (Arrangements Chair)

❏ Form receiving line. (Event Chair)

❏ Circulate as much as you can while still enforcing the agenda, or designate someone to watch the clock for you. (Arrangements Chair)

❏ Have guests sign in, if appropriate. (Invitation Chair)

❏ For last-minute cancellations, fill in no-shows at prominent tables with volunteer staff. (Arrangements Chair)

❏ Have a ribbon-cutting ceremony, if appropriate. (Arrangements Chair)

❑ End the event at a specific time. (Arrangements Chair)

❑ Have copies of your guest list available for future use. (Invitation Chair)

Month Eight

(Within two weeks after the event)

❑ Follow up immediately with donors and key event participants. (Donations Chair)

❑ Send a press release highlighting the event's success, goals reached, active participants and donors. Include photos. (Public Relations Chair)

❑ Hold event team wrap-up meeting, while details of the event are fresh. (Event Chair)

Month Nine

(One month after the event)

❑ Take care of thank-you notes and calls. (Invitation Chair)

❑ Update Web site. (Public Relations Chair)

❑ Critique the event. (Event Chair)

❑ Begin planning next event. (Event Chair)

Month Ten

(Two months after the event)

❑ Set up the calendar for a new project. (Event Chair)

❑ Update Web site. (Public Relations Chair)

Forms and Outlines

Status Report

Duplicate this form for each chair and for yourself. Use it to monitor each committee status, monthly, periodically, or at each committee meeting. Have the chair list the committee's responsibilities for that period, who is in charge of each, the deadline, budget, and status at the time of each report. After the event, you will have a running time line for the next event team to use in planning. Here is a sample report. The blank one follows.

Status Report
(refer to monthly calendar)

Chair Person: Food and Drink   Lori O'Connor
Event: MS Costume Ball
Current Date: April 10, 2000
Event Date: October 10, 2000

Item	Responsible Person	Due Date	Status	Budget
Solicit proposals from caterers and other vendors	Helen Lippincott	4/30/00	2 bids received, 1 outstanding	-0-

---

Forms and Outlines *(continued)*

Status Report
(refer to monthly calendar)

Chair Person:
Event:
Current Date:
Event Date:

Item	Responsible Person	Due Date	Status	Budget

Staging Timetable for Day of Event

Duplicate the blank timetable form for each committee chair. Have each chair list chronologically every item that must be completed on the day of the event, with the appropriate time for completion. Here is a sample. The blank form follows.

Time	What Happens
	Staging Timetable
	Decorations picked up from suppliers
	Balloons delivered
	Garage opens
	Kitchen items delivered
	Live auction props delivered
	Setup begins
	Beverage delivered
	Food delivered
	Auction items delivered
	Registration table set
	Kitchen set
	Bar set
	Decorations complete and final
	Coffee set
	Registration set
	Food table set
	Silent auction set
	Hot food goes on food table
	Music and dancing opens
	Registration opens
	Silent auction opens
	Auctioneer arrives
	5-minute warning for closing of Table 1 (Getaways)
	Check-out set
	Table 1 closes; bid sheets to check-out
	5-minute warning for closing of Table 2 (Services)
	Table 2 closes; bid sheets to check-out
	Check-out opens to attendees
	Registration closes
	Last call for beer and wine at bar

(continued next page)

Forms and Outlines *(continued)*

Staging Timetable *(continued)*

Time	What Happens
	Last call for raffle tickets
	End of beverage service
	Raffle closes
	Raffle winner envelope w/cash to podium
	Ask guests to pull chairs to stage area for live auction
	Sale table closes (discounted items that didn't receive any bids on Tables 1 or 2). Bid sheets to check-out
	Chair takes microphone to say thank-you
	Raffle winner chosen before opening of live auction
	Live auction begins
	Live auction closes
	Check-out continues
	Cleanup
	Garage closes

Staging Timetable

Time	What Happens

Forms and Outlines *(continued)*

Sample Thank-You Notes

To sponsor

Dear [Event Sponsor]*:*

    I am writing on behalf of the [XYZ Company] *to thank you for your generous donation of* [item] *to the* [event name]. *You truly helped make this event a success. The money raised at the* [event] *will* [help in some specific way].

    *We are pleased to announce that with your assistance, we were able to reach our goal of $*_____ *and hope to top that with our second Annual Event.*

    Again, thank you for your sponsorship. If you would be interested in participating next year on the event team, please contact me.

                    Sincerely,

                    _____

                    (Title)

To donor

Dear [$ Donor]:

I am writing on behalf of [XYZ Company] to thank you for your generous donation to the worthwhile cause of [name of cause]. You truly helped make this event a success. The money raised will assist [someone in some specific way].

We are pleased to announce that with your assistance, we were able to reach our goal of $_____ and hope to top that with our second Annual Event.

Again, thank you for your generous donation. If you would be interested in participating next year on the event team, please contact me.

Sincerely,

_____
(Title)

To event team member

Dear [name of member]:

Thank you for making the [name of event] a success. It is rewarding to write this note, knowing that together we have made a difference. I look forward to begin work on next year's event and hope to have you on the team.

Keep in touch.

Sincerely,

_____
(Title)

Forms and Outlines *(continued)*

Outline for Each Chair's Post-Event Written Report

Chair _____ Date _____

List below the name of each subcommittee, its chair, the responsibilities of the sub-committee, its budget, and members.

Subcommittees	Chair	Responsibilities	Budget	Committee Members

Describe how you think your committee handled its responsibilities:

_____

_____

_____

_____

_____

Your suggestions for the future:

_____

_____

_____

_____

_____

Attach copies of documents (such as contracts and invoices) and samples of completed projects, where appropriate (invitations, programs, news releases, and so forth).

Agenda for Post-Event Core Committee Meeting

- All chairs summarize their written reports.
- Collect all the reports and file in a binder or this workbook for next year.
- Record additional comments on written reports.
- Brainstorm ways to make each aspect of event stronger.
- If you are supporting a charity, encourage committee members to talk about the charity and the event within the community during the year to "keep it alive."
- Set a date for the next charity event for the following year.

Public Relations Chair

Responsibilities

- Create and place all public relations materials, including news and feature articles, calendar announcements, public service announcements, and print advertising.
- Respond to news media inquiries.
- Act as liaison with public relations representative for other key entities associated with the event, such as the benefiting charity, celebrity speaker, entertainer or spokesperson, major donor, and major event site.

Qualifications

- Ideally, some journalism or public relations experience; at a minimum, strong writing ability.
- Access to computer, with proficiency in word processing and, ideally, proficiency in a database program such as Microsoft Access or FileMaker Pro, and/or a spreadsheet program such as Microsoft Excel.
- Access to e-mail, fax, telephones.

Other Members of Public Relations Committee

- People with media experience who have and can make contacts.
- Phoners/researchers to assist in compiling media lists, make calls, and staff a press desk, if the event will attract on-site media attention.
- Volunteer professional "voice" to record public service ads, if available.

Conducting a Public Relations Campaign

Begin your PR effort by compiling a list of media contacts at newspapers, magazines, radio stations, TV stations, and relevant Internet sites. Scale the scope of your list to the nature and newsworthiness of event. For example, for a private high school dinner/auction, focus on local media, especially community newspapers and local cable channels; for a major gala with a national celebrity speaker or honoree, consider nearby big-city and national outlets, as well. Sources for media contacts include:

- Personal contacts.
- Media directories available at libraries. Such directories include *Bacon's Media Directory, Gale Directory of Publications and Broadcast Media, Gebbie Press All-in-One Directory,* and *Working Press of the Nation.*
- Local government community service or press relations offices.
- Internet listings.
- Telephone directory.

Your media list should be maintained in a computerized database, so you can easily generate media lists, mailing labels, and so forth. Confirm, update, and expand on listings information with a call to the media outlet; personnel change frequently. Reconfirm or update information every several months and just before making a major distribution.

Construct a calendar of when you will send press releases and other material to each type of media contact, depending in part on when you want the publicity to appear and what lead time the particular contact requires (ranges from a day or less for daily newspapers up to two or three months for some magazines).

Write or collect all materials that will be distributed to the media. Materials may include any of the following:

- Press release.
- Calendar announcement.
- Fact sheet about your company or auxiliary.
- Promotional material on big-name speaker or entertainer.
- Charity brochure (if one is available from the charity you are supporting).
- Picture of a company representative with the charity spokesperson.
- Picture of someone being helped by the cause you are supporting.
- Public service announcements.

Distribute materials according to your distribution calendar. Follow up personally with as many media outlets as possible, starting with those most important to your event.

Coordinate with the Invitation and Program Chair on substantive contents for the event program. (See the Invitation and Program Chair material, if you are going to be editor of the event program and will depend on the Invitation and Program Chair only for advertising.)

- Include a quotation from someone in your organization.
- End the release with three hatch marks (# # #) or the notation -30-, to indicate the copy is complete.
- If the release runs to two pages, at the bottom of the first page, write "—more—". On the second page, in the top left corner, place a slug—one or two words that identify the story, and put "ADD 1" or "PAGE 2" on the next line down. Skip two lines and finish the release.
- Double-check to make sure (do not guess or assume) the spelling of everyone's name and title is correct in the release. This point is critical.

Checklist for a News Advisory or Calendar Item

- A news advisory is a one-page "quickie" sent to print and electronic media to alert them to an upcoming event. It is the bare bones of a press release, limited to who, what, when, where, and why.

Checklist for Photographs and Videos

- Whenever possible, send a photograph with your release.
- Show action in the photograph. A CEO wielding a hammer on a home for Habitat for Humanity is going to make the photo editor happier than a shot of two men in suits shaking hands. Include animals or children in the picture, if plausible. Move in close to subjects. Many newspapers use the "dime rule." Whenever possible, make faces larger than a dime.

- Ask the cause you're supporting if any photographs are available.

- Although you can hire photographers, look for an experienced photographer who is a member of your committee or broader organization.

- Do not write on the back of a photograph. Write a caption and identify all people, from left to right. Attach the caption to the bottom of the photo, so the information is visible from the front.

- Send photos or videos with press releases to television stations and cable channels. Visuals are crucial in television, and TV can be a powerful source in promoting the event.

- Radio and TV stations are becoming more amenable to using videos and audiotapes. Talk to the stations and find out if they will accept audio or video two-minute news releases, and even the outtakes from preparing video releases. Sometimes the station will even be willing to produce a tape for you.

Checklist for On-Line Media and Web Sites

- Establish a Web site for your event, either as part of your organization's existing Web site or as a free-standing site. Find an organization member (or an Internet-savvy offspring of a member) to design and mount the site, if you are not experienced at that task. Perhaps you can get a professional to donate Web-site work. Your site should both inform and "sell" the public, as appropriate to your event. You can, for example, promote the benefiting charity, solicit auction items, take ticket reservations, display auction or prize items, and post directions. If you have a comprehensive Web site, be sure to provide its URL in all media materials.

- If your event or charity has a logo, be sure you have it available in electronic form.

- Be aware of on-line media relevant to your event, such as community bulletin boards, arts calendars, Chamber of Commerce Web sites, and the like. Ask these sites to list your event, display your logo, and if appropriate, provide a link to your site.

- Be sure your benefiting-charity site includes a reference to your event and a link to your event site.

Checklist for Public Service Announcements

The Federal Communications Commission requires TV and radio stations to give a certain amount of free air time as a public service. To capitalize on this free advertisement opportunity, send your local stations public service announcements they will want to air.

- Write two PSAs to send to local radio and TV stations. Ten- and thirty-second PSAs are the most common for these messages, which serve as free commercials.

- Mail several copies of each PSA to radio and TV stations. If you send an audio or video cassette, include several copies of the script with the tape.

- Follow up with a phone call. Ask the station to air your PSA every day for two weeks before your event, to get maximum impact. If you are involved in a long-term campaign, you will need to send fresh PSAs to the radio stations from time to time.

- PSAs have a specific format. See the samples later in this handbook.

- Use organization letterhead.
- Triple space (except between ANNCR: and the body of the message).
- Use very wide margins.
- Always write in capital letters.
- Your name and phone number are typed in the top right corner, in case the station has any questions.
- The next number below that on the left margin is the time it takes to read the commercial. For a ten-second spot, it will read :10. For a thirty-second spot, it will read :30. Be realistic when you time your spots.
- The "Kill Date" is the last date the PSA should be read on the air. In this case, it should be the date the event is to take place.
- "ANNCR" is the announcer, or disc jockey, who will read the PSA over the air.
- Include hyphens between each digit of a phone number.
- The last number—in parentheses ( )—is the number of words in the text.

Calendar

Establishing Your Calendar

Many major events take a year to plan. For either a yearlong campaign or a major event, complete the groundwork listed in the calendar for Months One and Two at least six months before the event.

Many events can be pulled off with flair only a few months ahead of time. You may even put on an event Fast!—within a few weeks. Whether you plan to do a yearlong campaign, a midsized event, or a Fast! event, you must follow some basic steps. The following calendar contains the fundamental public rela-

Month Six

(Two months before the event)

❑ Meet with key officials or community business leaders, possibly over lunch, to discuss charity and stimulate more interest and involvement.

❑ Send a press release about the event accompanied by a photo of key people in your organization with the endorsing celebrity, spokesperson, or charity sponsor.

❑ Distribute PSA material to electronic media.

❑ Update Status Report.

Month Seven

(One month before the event)

❑ Send out press releases and public service announcements about the event, stating location and event goals.

❑ Continue to distribute PSA material.

❑ Two weeks before the event, send out a News Advisory or Calendar item for inclusion in wire service and newspaper calendars. (see sample)

❑ Update Web page.

❑ Update Status Report.

One week before the event

❑ Send a final press release to media you are targeting. Include any new noteworthy information, such as celebrities or dignitaries expected to attend.

❑ Make follow-up calls to media five days before the event. Keep calling until you have definite answers, but be polite and non-confrontational.

❑ Arrange for celebrity interviews on day of event.

❑ Set up a special room or quiet site for possible interviews on day of event.

☐ Make final television and radio pitch the day before the event.

☐ Find out and fulfill any broadcast-media needs, such as electrical outlets or an elevated stage.

☐ If audio or video tapes are requested by the media or others, make certain these arrangements are made.

☐ Update Status Report

Day of the event

☐ Get mobile phones to keep in touch with the media and other committee members.

☐ Allow extra time, because something will always go wrong.

☐ Prepare a list of expected media for the registration tables.

☐ Make certain you have a name tag to identify yourself to the incoming media.

☐ Set up media registration table with press kits and media sign-in sheet. Do not overstuff the press kit with unnecessary material that will end up on the floor. Include a press release, a fast fact sheet, a photograph or two, information on the auction items, brief information on the participating charity, and biographical information on any celebrities involved.

☐ Know the names, titles, and spellings of all key participants. Include correct pronunciations.

☐ Sit at press table, if appropriate. Otherwise, make yourself readily available to answer media inquiries.

☐ Take careful handwritten notes or use a tape recorder to record important talks from the podium. If you cannot do this task, assign somebody else to do it.

☐ Display a positive, confident, professional, relaxed demeanor.

Month Eight

(Within two weeks after the event)

☐ Complete post-event written report for Event Chair.

☐ Send a press release highlighting the event's success, goals reached, active participants, and donors. Include photos.

Month Nine

(One month after the event)

☐ Take care of thank-you notes and calls.

☐ Update Web site.

☐ Critique the event.

☐ Begin planning next event.

Month Ten

(Two months after the event)

☐ Set up the calendar for a new project.

☐ Update Web site.

A Gala Event!

Forms and Outlines

Status Report

Duplicate this form and submit it monthly or periodically to your event chair. Here is a sample for Month One. The blank form follows.

Status Report
(refer to monthly calendar)

Chair Person: Public Relations   Ellen Simon
Event: MS Costume Ball
Current Date: April 10, 2000
Event Date: October 10, 2000

Item	Responsible Person	Due Date	Status	Budget
Assemble a media contact list	Ann Johnson	4/30/00	TV list ready, radio pending	$50.00
Establish a Web site	Bill Pope	4/30/00	Up and running	$250.00

Status Report
(refer to monthly calendar)

Chair Person: Public Relations
Event:
Current Date:
Event Date:

Item	Responsible Person	Due Date	Status	Budget

Media Contact Information List for Newspapers and Magazines

Name of newspaper or magazine _____

When published _____
(e.g., daily Mon-Sat; weekly on Wednesdays; last day of month)

Deadlines _____
(e.g., 4 p.m. day before publication; Mondays at 9 a.m.; 2nd week of prior month)

Telephone number _____

Address _____

Fax number _____

E-mail address _____

Name and phone number
of lifestyle editor _____

Name and phone number
of entertainment editor _____

Name and phone number
of business editor _____

Name and phone number
of community news/community
calendar editor _____

Name and phone number
of photo editor _____

Preferred contact for this event _____

Preferred method of delivery _____
(e.g., fax, e-mail, hand delivery)

Preferred photo format _____
(e.g., black-and-white or color, glossy or matte, digital)

Forms and Outlines *(continued)*

Sample Skeleton of a Press Release

NAME OF CONTACT, TITLE
NAME OF COMPANY (IF NOT ON LETTERHEAD)
TELEPHONE NUMBER   FOR IMMEDIATE RELEASE

HEADLINE FOR THE PRESS RELEASE

City, State, Date—Cover who, what, when, where, and why in the first paragraph or, occasionally, the first two paragraphs. Present the information in short, easy-to-read sentences.

The second paragraph can be a continuation of the information in the first sentence, or it can be an elaboration. This is a good place to detail the reason the event is taking place.

A quotation from someone in your organization can go next. Make sure you spell the person's name correctly and include the person's title.

Include a paragraph about the charity or cause you are supporting.

Always end the text by giving the name and phone number of the person the media can contact for more information.

# # #

Sample Public Service Announcement

Your Name

Phone Number

:30

KILL DATE: **DATE OF EVENT**

ANNCR:

HELP UNITE THE BLIND WITH LEADER DOGS. **THE COMPANY NAME** WILL SPONSOR A BLACK TIE DINNER TO BENEFIT **LEADER DOGS FOR THE BLIND,** A NONPROFIT ORGANIZATION THAT PROVIDES GUIDE DOGS TO THE BLIND. THE DINNER WILL BE **DATE, TIME, AND LOCATION.** GET INVOLVED BY CALLING **0-0-0, 0-0-0-0** FOR DETAILS.

(00) **Number of words in text**

Forms and Outlines *(continued)*

Media Sign-In Sheet for Day of Event

Media Sign-In Sheet for Day of Event				
Name	Organization	Address	Phone	E-Mail

Charity Liaison Chair

Responsibilities

- Act as a liaison between the event team and the benefiting charity's headquarters.
- Obtain information and materials from the charity headquarters as the event is developed.
- Line up a charity spokesperson to publicize your event and speak at it.
- Relay to the other chairs all information gleaned from the national charity headquarters.
- Encourage a representative of the charity to attend every event team meeting.

Working with the Charity

Contact the public relations or marketing department of the benefiting charity and ask what material the department can provide you. Often the charity will have brochures, videos, slide presentations, and fact sheets.

If you receive a video, ask for a written script of the tape. If the charity office sends a slide presentation, ask that the slides be identified, so you can make sure they're in the right order. Ask for a script with notations of where each slide should be used. If the charity does have slides but no prepared slide presentation, ask that the contents of each slide be identified, so you can prepare your own show.

Inquire about a celebrity spokesperson. Often a national charity already has a celebrity spokesperson associated with its cause. Work with the headquarters to place your event on the spokesperson's calendar of appearances so he or she can promote your event at other appearances and lend the support of his or her friends and colleagues.

Network with the charity. Get to know the charity board of directors or advisory board, perhaps by taking board members to lunch or dinner. Fostering friendships among board members makes it easier to ask the charity how to do something and easier to understand how the charity works. It also gives you the opportunity to introduce your group to these often-influential people.

Contribute to the event mailing list. Include people who might be interested in your project. Ask the charity for its list, or the portion of the list covering your area. Brainstorm with your event team and make a list of names, addresses, and phone numbers of people who come to mind when you think about the charity. Begin the list with clients, friends, and neighbors who are active, outgoing, and community-service oriented. Also, make a list of city officials, local business owners, and interest groups. For a fund-raising campaign, the list could look like this:

- Rotary Clubs
- Chamber of Commerce
- Museum guilds
- Hospital auxiliaries

- Women's clubs
- Lions Clubs
- Philanthropic organizations
- Civic Clubs
- Professional organizations

Some of these organizations may already support the cause you have selected. Great! You can contact the local chapter and ask for help with your event. Discuss your overlapping interests and coordinate efforts.

Collect existing mailing lists. Obtaining access to a variety of organizations' mailing lists is a powerful reason to include people on your event team who are already active in the community. Ask all members on the event team to contribute the membership rosters of any groups they belong to. It's far easier for a member of the country club to ask permission to use the list for a charity than for a stranger to come in and request use of the list.

If your event is national in scope, get people from different states to refer you to individuals experienced in fund-raising. It is essential to bring in people who know that area. For example, if your corporation has decided to put on a national function, call groups on your contact list in each state. Explain that you are looking for a community leader to serve on a national committee. If the executive director of the group you are calling does not have the time to serve, ask that person to recommend someone else who could.

Other tasks include:

- Invite the senior representative of the charity to attend the event as a guest to sit at the head table.
- Coordinate with the Public Relations Chair to provide information about the event to the charity newsletter.
- Include on the event program a presentation of funds to the charity, or if the amount can't be determined until

Forms and Outlines

Status Report

Duplicate this form and submit it monthly or periodically to your event chair. Here is a sample for Month One. The blank form follows.

Status Report
(refer to monthly calendar)

Chair Person: Charity Liaison   Neil Hughes
Event: MS Costume Ball
Current Date: April 10, 2000
Event Date: October 10, 2000

Item	Responsible Person	Due Date	Status	Budget
Form committee	Neil Hughes	4/30/00	All members in place	-0-
Contact charity headquarters	Julianne Bodnar	4/30/00	Talked to Dean Maury, president. They will supply media mailing list, area members list, schedule Tarzan as speaker.	-0-

Status Report
(refer to monthly calendar)

Chair Person: Charity Liaison
Event:
Current Date:
Event Date:

Item	Responsible Person	Due Date	Status	Budget

Donations and Sponsors Chair

Responsibilities

- Underwrite the event by obtaining donations and sponsor support.

Qualifications

- Sufficient aggressiveness and thick skin to ask directly for goods and services and not be discouraged by sometimes getting "no" for an answer.

How to Find Sponsors

Your basic objective is to get businesses and individuals to donate as many goods and services as possible for your organization to use to stage the event. In the volunteer world, rarely does a fund-raising project get allotted a budget from the outset. Costs of elements of the event can be determined, though, and are helpful when arranging for underwriting. Ideally, donations

❑ Sponsor seminars of interest to the public or to civic or hobby associations (e.g., Junior League, garden clubs).

❑ Follow up your contacts network with information and opportunities for participation.

❑ Continue to contact local companies for contributions and sponsorships.

❑ Continue to contact active members of the community, interest groups, media, city officials, and key community leaders.

❑ Update Status Report.

Month Four

(Four months before major event)

❑ Conduct public speaking engagements and seminars.

❑ Update Status Report.

Month Five

(Thee months before major event)

❑ Continue speaking to special interest groups.

❑ Continue to collect auction items.

❑ Update Status Report.

Month Six

(Two months before the event)

❑ Continue to network with outside groups through public speaking engagements.

❑ Continue to target business and community organizations, key city officials, and interest groups.

❑ Update Status Report.

Month Seven

(One month before the event)

❑ Keep in touch with business and community organizations, key city officials, interest groups.

❑ Step up your push for collecting auction items. Work hand-in-hand with the Auction Chair and the Event Chair to discuss what is needed and where you are in the collection process.

❑ Update Status Report.

One week before the event

❑ All auction items should be picked up and tagged. Description of any last-minute items should be given to the Program Chair for insertion into program.

❑ All committee members should know their responsibilities for day of event.

Day of the event

❑ Circulate as much as you can.

❑ Recognize the sponsors, donors, and your other key contacts personally.

Month Eight

(Within two weeks after the event)

❑ Event Chair collects Status Reports.

❑ Follow up immediately with donors and key event participants.

Month Nine

(One month after the event)

❑ Take care of thank-you notes and calls.

❑ Begin planning next event.

Month Ten

(Two months after the event)

❑ Set up the calendar for a new project.

Sponsorship Form					
Name	Address	Phone	Fax	E-mail	Donation

Forms and Outlines

Status Report

Duplicate this form and submit it monthly or periodically to your event chair. Here is a sample for Month One. The blank form follows.

Status Report
(refer to monthly calendar)

Chair Person: Donations and Sponsors   Kris Coons
Event: MS Costume Ball
Current Date: April 10, 2000
Event Date: October 10, 2000

Item	Responsible Person	Due Date	Status	Budget
Form committee	Kris Coons	4/30/00	All members in place	-0-
Begin list of key business and community leaders	Jennifer Hughes	4/30/00	All real estate names in database, working on builders.	$50.00

Status Report
(refer to monthly calendar)

Chair Person: Donations and Sponsors
Event:
Current Date:
Event Date:

Item	Responsible Person	Due Date	Status	Budget

Arrangements and Logistics Chair

Responsibilities

- Select and contract for the event location.
- Arrange and oversee all logistics concerning the location.
- Coordinate with other chairs involved at the location, including Food and Drink, Entertainment and Auction, Decorations, and Cleanup.

Qualifications

- Some experience in contracting for goods and services.

Selecting the Location

The location will be one of the most important elements of the event. A bad site can ruin an otherwise well-planned event. You must first evaluate sites to determine which are capable of meeting the needs of your event. In many cases, you must coordinate with the Food and Drink Chair. Here are some factors that may be relevant for your particular event:

- Size of the room or facility (the banquet room at a small hotel or inn may not accommodate a seated dinner for 500).

- Capacity and style of available food service.

- Atmosphere of the facility. (Is it too stuffy, too casual, or too formal in relation to the event?)

- If the site is at a restaurant, is the kitchen adequate? Will there be separate staff assigned to your event? If so, how many? If you wish to bring in donated wines for the dinner, is there a corkage fee? If so, how much? Will the restaurant wait staff have to carry your food through a dining room filled with other patrons? If so, your food may be only lukewarm. Is the restaurant smoke free or cigar friendly?

- Ease of access, both in terms of distance your attendees must travel and the relative convenience or inconvenience they will encounter upon arrival. (Is it easy to locate? Does it have sufficient nearby parking? Covered entrance, if it is raining?)

- Is it accessible to the physically challenged?

- Available stage, power, lighting, dance floor, movie screen, warm-up room, etc.

- Available on the date or alternate date you need?

- No other simultaneous event in conflict? (If you are raising money to cure lung cancer, you wouldn't want to share a hotel with a tobacco company sales meeting.)

- Priced within the event budget? What is the wait service tip, if any?

- If located in a large building or in a below surface room, can cellular phones and pagers work properly? . . . important for some professionals such as physicians or corporation executives. If site is wireless unfriendly, make certain telephones are readily accessible.

Contracting for the Location

Once you select a location, you must contract to ensure it in fact does meet your needs, and there are no misunderstandings that could intrude on the event. During contract negotiation, you must examine the site with a fine-toothed comb and contemplate what could go wrong. For example, are the walls of the banquet room permanent, or are they pull-across dividers, and if the latter, is a loud event booked next door? Does the union contract with hotel service personnel expire the day before your event? Is the Sheraton hotel contracted to become a Marriott by the time of your event?

Negotiation time is also the time to bargain for the extras you need that could improve the event. Can you get a free guest room for the featured speaker? How about complimentary coffee for guests at the end of the evening?

A contract should include the following elements:

- Complete listing and cost (or specified no-cost) of all items to be supplied by the site, including the physical locations, equipment, and personnel. Be certain costs include all taxes, gratuities, coat checks, service charges, or minimum room charges.

- The times during which these items will be available without additional charge, and the additional charge for extra time. Be certain you have sufficient advance access to the site, for decoration and setup.

- Deposit and payment schedule.

- Last date by which event can be canceled or postponed and deposit returned.

- Last date by which event can be canceled or postponed with loss of deposit, but no additional charge.

- Provision for payment of physical damage caused by the event or its guests.
- Provision for resolving issues of damage caused by the site to event or its guests.
- Cleanup requirements, including deadlines. (For example, you might have to have all presentation equipment and materials removed from your afternoon meeting by 5:00, so the hotel can prepare for a 7:00 dinner.)
- Identification of one contact person for the site and one for the event (presumably you) to handle all arrangements and issues. (You don't want to have to chase a lot of different site people, and you don't want other event people going around you with special requests.)
- Provisions for valet parking?
- Provisions for floral arrangements and costs.
- If needed, cost and provisions for entertainment.
- If a tent is needed to extend a site, what are the charges?

Other Logistical Tasks

Once the location is selected and contracted for, you must see to the other logistical details that involve the location.

- Arrange parking, if necessary.
- Coordinate with the Decorating and Entertainment committees to make sure site personnel or the appropriate committee takes care of everything in the physical space where the event will be held, including decorating on the day of the event and seating and space for speakers or entertainment.
- Make certain the room is open as necessary for setup and the event.
- Make sure audiovisual needs are met.

- Rent mobile phones or pagers as necessary. Make certain they work properly at site.
- Take charge of lighting.
- Take charge of room temperature.
- Have access to and control (including the "off" button) of any piped-in music.

Calendar

Establishing Your Calendar

Many major events take a year to plan. As soon as the type of event is determined, site selection must be undertaken. Large and attractive sites typically book many months, or even years, in advance. For either a yearlong campaign or a major event, complete the groundwork listed in the calendar for Months One and Two at least six months before the event.

Many events can be pulled off with flair only a few months ahead of time. You may even put on an event Fast!—within a few weeks. Whether you plan to do a yearlong campaign, a mid-sized event, or a Fast! event, the Arrangements and Logistics Chair must follow some basic steps. The following calendar contains the fundamental arrangements and logistics checkpoints for almost any event, although the months may have to be condensed to fit your timetable. Some listed items will involve only checking with another committee chair to confirm that arrangements touching on your areas of responsibility are in order.

A Gala Event!

Calendar Checklist for a Yearlong Campaign or Major Event

Month One

(Seven to ten months before major event)

☐ Customize this calendar to your specific needs.

☐ Form Arrangements and Logistics Committee.

☐ Compile requirements for event.

☐ Develop list of possible locations and make initial telephone inquiries.

☐ Visit possible locations.

☐ Coordinate with Event Chair on selection of an event site.

☐ Update Status Report each month or periodically as needed.

Month Two

(At least six months before major event)

☐ Complete contractual arrangements with event location.

☐ Determine audiovisual needs.

☐ If auction planned, check out room to store items.

☐ Update Status Report.

Month Three

(Five months before major event)

☐ Continue to make physical arrangements for the event, such as firming up location details, overnight-room needs, food, entertainment, audiovisual needs, and self or valet parking.

☐ Update Status Report.

Month Four

(Four months before major event)

- [ ] Select and order souvenirs.
- [ ] Maintain contact with location representative to make certain all is well.
- [ ] Update Status Report.

Month Five

(Three months before major event)

- [ ] Follow up with arrangements for catering, rentals, and other physical details.
- [ ] Update Status Report.

Month Six

(Two months before the event)

- [ ] Follow up event arrangements, such as audiovisual. Keep in mind any alternative measures for mix-ups of any kind.
- [ ] Firm up plans for how your event will conclude.
- [ ] Obtain all necessary insurance, sales-tax paperwork, tent licenses, liquor license, or street closure permit.
- [ ] Update Status Report

Month Seven

(One month before the event)

- [ ] Confirm speaker and entertainment. With Event Chair, arrange for a backup speaker in case an emergency prevents the first choice from appearing.
- [ ] Prepare a realistic agenda/schedule for speakers, participants, and entertainment with specific time limits, and confirm with participants. Coordinate this agenda with Event Chair.

❑ Help prepare a printed program, if appropriate.

❑ Be prepared for the unexpected, such as bad weather or speaker cancellation. Have a contingency plan for each, such as rental facilities for a tent.

❑ Reserve mobile phones.

❑ Plan for medical professional, such as company nurse, to be on hand for emergencies during the event.

❑ Update Status Report.

One week before the event

❑ Confirm refreshments, audio equipment, seating, restrooms, first aid, photographer, supplies, flowers, decorations, entertainment, and so forth.

❑ Finalize parking arrangements.

❑ Prepare a step-by-step agenda for the big day. Include all pertinent information on a staging guide. (Refer to p. 58 of *Gala!* for sample.)

❑ Conduct a dress rehearsal of the event with core committee members from start to finish. If that is not possible, at least check the sound system.

❑ If possible, have the keynote speaker rehearse. If this is not feasible, make sure he or she knows what to do from the moment of arrival through departure.

❑ Confirm that your stage guide is realistic. Double-check times and set time limits for speakers, entertainment, participants, and the core committee.

❑ Confirm on-site storage arrangements for decorations, auction items, and so forth in advance of event.

❑ Update Status Report.

Day of the event

☐ Allow extra time, because something will always go wrong.

☐ Provide transportation for dignitaries and guest speakers who need it.

☐ Distribute confirmed agenda to keynote speakers, participants, and core committee. Make sure they know what to do.

☐ Display table assignments at the entry.

☐ Be sure greeters or ushers are in place.

☐ Form receiving line.

☐ Circulate as much as you can while still enforcing the agenda, or designate someone to watch the clock for you.

☐ Have guests sign in, if appropriate.

☐ For last-minute cancellations, fill in no-shows at prominent tables with volunteer staff.

☐ If name tags are displayed on registration table, gather them up once the program begins. There is no need for guests to peruse the names of no-show guests.

☐ End the event at the specified time.

☐ Help cleanup committee check for lost items. If any, pre-designated person on cleanup committee should collect and take home or to their office. Make certain all chairs know the name of the collection person, so frantic telephone calls from guests can be responded to properly and accurately.

Month Eight

(Within two weeks after event)

☐ Complete post-event written report for Event Chair.

Months Nine-Ten

(One-two months after event)

☐ Take care of thank-you notes and calls.

☐ Submit suggestions for fine-tuning next year's event.

☐ Set up calendar for a new project.

A Gala Event!

Forms and Outlines

Status Report

Duplicate this form for each of your subchair people and for yourself. Use it to monitor each committee's status monthly, periodically, or at each committee meeting. Have the chair list the committee's responsibilities for that period, who is in charge of each, the deadline, budget, and status at the time of each report. After the event, you will have a running time line for the next event team to use in planning. Here is a sample report. The blank one follows.

Status Report
(refer to monthly calendar)

Chair Person: Arrangements and Logistics   Julianne Bodnar
Event: MS Costume Ball
Current Date: April 10, 2000
Event Date: October 10, 2000

Item	Responsible Person	Due Date	Status	Budget
Form Arrangements and Logistics Committee	Julianne Bodnar	4/30/00	All positions filled	-0-
Develop list of possible locations and make initial telephone inquiries	Neil Hughes	4/15/00	5 locations identified, 3 owe Neil callbacks	
Visit possible locations	Neil & Julianne	5/1/00	Appointments scheduled with 2 hotels	

Status Report
(refer to monthly calendar)

Chair Person: Arrangements and Logistics
Event:
Current Date:
Event Date:

Item	Responsible Person	Due Date	Status	Budget

Food and Drink Chair

Responsibilities

- Arrange for food and beverages for the event.
- Arrange for liquor license, if required.
- Decide how much food and drink will be needed.
- Find restaurants, caterers, or people to donate food and drinks.
- Arrange for transportation of food and drink to event location, if necessary.
- Arrange a "tasting" party for a limited number of the committee before the event.

Qualifications

- Experienced host or hostess.
- Must know culinary requirements of target guest list and theme of event.

Choosing Food and Beverages

For many events, the food and beverages will be the most expensive item. In many cases, the quality of the food will be what guests first consider, when asked if they enjoyed the event. Accordingly, the food and beverages must be carefully chosen to fit the budget, the theme, and the style of the event and must be of high quality, whether it be beef Wellington or hot dogs. You must work with the Arrangements Chair at the outset, because choice of event location is likely to determine whether the location will also provide food or you will need a caterer or other food provider.

Principal tasks in the planning process vary, depending on the nature of your event, but will include at least some of the following:

- Select food provider and menu within a budget.
- Arrange for liquor license, if required.
- Arrange for any required health permit, if your event will be selling food.
- Decide how much food and drink will be needed.
- Find restaurants, caterers, or people to donate food and drinks.
- Arrange for transportation of food and drink to event location, if necessary.
- Arrange for food and drink service, including flatware, serving dishes, napkins, and staff, which may be provided by a caterer or hotel food service.
- Arrange a tasting for the relevant committee members before the event.

The Contract

All arrangements for food and beverage service should be specified in a contract with the site or caterer. The contract should include these points:

- Exactly what will be served (specific menu) and poured (kinds of beverage and brand names, whether premium or house), as well as portion sizes. (For example, eight-ounce steak, 1.5 ounces of liquor in drinks.)

- How and where guests will be served. (For example, round tables of eight, two buffet tables, three service bars, etc.)

- Service personnel. (For example, one waitperson per sixteen seats; one bartender per hundred guests, etc.)

- When and how service and cleanup will occur. (For example, service bars open 7-8 p.m., table service begins at 8:15 p.m., last table to be served not more than fifteen minutes after first table; all dishes and utensils to be removed from dining room prior to scraping.)

- How beverage service at tables will be handled. (Unless you direct otherwise, waitpersons usually refill glasses with bottled water or wine as often as they can, to drive up your cost; you may choose to limit the number of bottles per table.)

- The corkage charge, if you supply your own wines or specialty beverages. (Perhaps a California winemaker is donating the wine for your New York dinner raising money for a California-based charity.)

- The cost per person for food and the number of persons guaranteed. In setting the guarantee, you normally should reduce the expected attendance by five percent, but make sure more people can be accommodated, if necessary. Food service usually will set up for about five percent more than the guarantee. If your event may have additional walk-up attendance, determine if extras can be accommodated. (Is there space in the room? Are tables and chairs available? Can some food be prepared on short notice?)

- What type of beverage-ware will be used, plastic or glass.

- The cost for beverages. The cost for beverages may variously be calculated in some combination of bottles consumed, drinks consumed, persons in attendance, and/or bartenders on duty. If you are having no-host bar service, arrange for the site to provide a cashier or have committee members sell drink tickets, in which case you will need to coordinate with the Logistics Chair and prepare to handle and account for money.

Beverage Planning

If you are providing the beverages and/or beverage service, you can estimate your requirements on these general principles:

- One liter of liquor serves twenty-two drinks at one and a half ounces per drink, or about seven or eight people.
- One bottle of wine serves six drinks at four ounces, which means partially filling the glasses. A bottle will yield five glasses, if you fill glasses more generously.
- One gallon of wine serves thirty-three drinks at four ounces each.
- Calculate two drinks per person for a one-hour cocktail hour, and remember most people forget where they leave their glasses and order a fresh drink. Make sure you have plenty of extra glasses, which, unless your event is extremely informal, should be glass, rather than paper or plastic.
- Have on hand bottled water, club soda, tonic water, soft drinks, and fruit juices.
- Minimize overcrowding and long lines by having several bar locations.

A Gala Event!

Calendar

Establishing Your Calendar

Many major events can take a year to plan. For either a yearlong campaign or a major event, complete the groundwork listed in the calendar for Months One and Two at least six months before the event.

Many events can be pulled off with flair only a few months ahead of time. You may even put on an event Fast!—within a few weeks. Whether you plan to do a yearlong campaign, a mid-sized event, or a Fast! event, you must follow some basic steps. The following calendar contains the fundamental food and drink checkpoints for almost any event, although the months may have to be condensed to fit your timetable.

Calendar Checklist for a Yearlong or Major Event

Month One

(Seven to ten months before major event)

❑ Form your committee.

❑ Decide what sort of food and refreshments will be served.

❑ Begin soliciting proposals from caterers and other vendors.

❑ Update Status Report.

Month Two

(At least six months before major event)

❑ Decide what sort of table linens, table service, and other physical arrangements fit the theme of your event.

❑ Update Status Report.

Month Three

(Five months before major event)

❏ Contact local companies for food or beverage contributions.

❏ Begin to finalize arrangements for food and beverage service.

❏ Update Status Report.

Month Four

(Four months before major event)

❏ Update Status Report.

Month Five

(Three months before major event)

❏ Follow up with arrangements for catering, rentals, and other physical details. Work with Arrangements Committee.

❏ Update Status Report.

Month Six

(Two months before the event)

❏ Follow up with caterers and/or beverage providers.

❏ Be prepared for the unexpected. For example, if you are having an outdoor event, how will the food be served in bad weather?

❏ Update Status Report.

Month Seven

(One month before the event)

❏ Have the hotel food service or caterer prepare and present a trial dinner for a small number of committee members.

☐ Prepare a realistic service agenda with the Arrangements Committee.

☐ Update Status Report.

One week before the event

☐ Reconfirm food and refreshments.

☐ Keep in daily contact with the caterer, for changes in the number of expected guests. Caterers will require you to give a "guarantee" by a specific date. After that date, numbers can only go up.

☐ Double check to see if there are any special requests for food, such as vegetarian, no salt, etc., and give to caterer.

☐ Obtain a mobile phone to stay in contact with others, because you may be in kitchen all night overseeing the food service. Don't expect to enjoy the meal casually with the guests.

☐ Update Status Report.

Day of the event

☐ Be organized, so you can start on time.

☐ Allow extra time, because something will always go wrong.

☐ Follow the confirmed staging guide.

☐ Make sure the caterer has all special requests for food.

☐ Check the bar setup for adequate amounts and kinds of liquor, wine, club soda, tonic water, soft drinks, fruit juices, and bottled water.

☐ Oversee the food service.

Month Eight

(Within two weeks after the event)

☐ Complete post-event written report for Event Chair.

☐ Follow up immediately with donors and key event participants.

☐ Hold event team wrap-up meeting, while details of the
event are fresh.

Month Nine

(One month after the event)

☐ Take care of thank-you notes and calls.

☐ Critique the event.

☐ Begin planning next event.

Month Ten

(Two months after the event)

☐ Set up the calendar for a new project.

Forms and Outlines

Status Report

Duplicate this form for each of your subchair people and for yourself. Use it to monitor each committee monthly, periodically, or at each committee meeting. Have the chair list the committee's responsibilities for that period, who is in charge of each, the deadline, budget, and status at the time of each report. After the event, you will have a running time line for the next event team to use in planning. Here is a sample report. The blank one follows.

Status Report
(refer to monthly calendar)

Chair Person: Food and Drink   Charles Reichmuth
Event: MS Costume Ball
Current Date: April 10, 2000
Event Date: October 10, 2000

Item	Responsible Person	Due Date	Status	Budget
Form Food and Drink Committee	Charles Reichmuth	4/30/00	All positions filled	-0-
Decide what sort of food and refreshments will be served	Scott McNeal	4/15/00	Discussed event theme with chair. Developed possible menu.	
Begin soliciting proposals from caterers and other vendors	Scott & Charles	5/1/00	Appointments scheduled with 2 caterers	

Status Report
(refer to monthly calendar)

Chair Person: Food and Drink
Event:
Current Date:
Event Date:

Item	Responsible Person	Due Date	Status	Budget

Decorating Chair

Responsibilities

- Acquire and set up the tables, flowers, and overall ambience.

Qualifications

- Artistic or design flair.

Planning the Décor

The Event Chair and Arrangements Committee will choose the overall event theme. The Decorating Committee will execute the theme. A local florist is a good choice for membership on the Decorating Committee, because a florist can steer you toward good centerpieces at affordable prices. Other good choices for committee membership include a local theater-set designer, gardeners, or a garden club award winner. It's possible for committee members to create the event centerpieces themselves, especially when gardens are in bloom. Consider selling the centerpieces at the event to cover their cost, with any profit donated to your designated charity.

Other important planning points include the following:

- Make sure the decorations are nonflammable, especially if candles are on the tables.

- Select, obtain, and distribute party favors. The Decorating Chair and the Donations Chair should put their heads together with the Entertainment Chair to find small, attractive, useful items that will coordinate with the event theme and tone. It would be a shame, for example, to send people home from an elegant black-tie evening with lifeless, unappealing gifts in a plain brown bag.

- Sometimes the entertainer serves as a natural tie-in to party favors or another part of the event. Famous people have been known to give samples of their perfume at promotional events, for example.

- If the speaker for the evening is an author, the party favor could be an autographed volume of the person's book purchased for a substantial bulk discount, if not donated by the author or publisher.

- If considering the use of large wall decorations or sets, work with the Arrangements Chair to be sure large or heavy items can be unloaded at the site loading dock or other suitable spot and transported through the building to the event room.

- Large wall or free-standing decorations should be securely attached or buttressed to avoid people bumping them down onto others—a possible litigation mishap.

- Coordinate with the Cleanup Chair for post-event removal of everything from the doilies under centerpieces to large movie-style sets.

Executing the Plan

The Decorating Committee typically has a very brief time to mount its decorations, often because the event site is available only hours before the guests arrive, and also because items often used in décor (flowers, ice) or favor bags (chocolate, fruit) often are fragile. Accordingly, the Decorating Chair must carefully plan how volunteers will be deployed in the final hours before the event, and how many volunteers will be needed. If the event site is not available at the appropriate time, another location may be needed to construct centerpieces, fill goody bags, and otherwise assemble decorations or giveaways. A truck, van, or SUV may be needed to move items. Even small goody bags can take up a great deal of space, if there are 500 of them.

Calendar

Establishing Your Calendar

Many major events can take a year to plan. For either a yearlong campaign or a major event, complete groundwork listed in the calendar for Months One and Two at least six months before the event.

Many events can be pulled off with flair only a few months ahead of time. You may even put on an event Fast!—within a few weeks. Whether you plan to do a yearlong campaign, a midsized event, or a Fast! event, the Decorating Chair must follow some basic steps. For the Decorating Chair, the amount of time required will depend primarily on the complexity of the decorations, not necessarily the size of the event. Elaborate outdoor sets for an exclusive garden party may take far longer than lavish floral centerpieces for a banquet seating 1,000. The following calendar contains the fundamental decorations checkpoints for almost any event, although the months may have to be condensed to fit your timetable.

Calendar Checklist for a Yearlong Campaign or Major Event

Months One-Three

(Five to ten months before major event)

❏ Form individual committee.

❏ Members of committee decide tablecloths, napkins, flowers, and centerpieces designed around the theme of the event.

❏ Meet with facility personnel on suggestions for your theme. They may have special contacts that will be helpful.

❏ Work with the Arrangements Chair to select favors or souvenirs for event. Order items promptly, because they may take months to produce.

❏ Check with Auction Chair to determine decorating needs for bidding tables.

❏ Update Status Report each month or periodically as needed.

Month Four

(Four months before major event)

❏ Make sure favors and souvenirs are on target for delivery at least one week before event, if not sooner.

❏ Meet with florist to discuss centerpieces.

❏ Check with Entertainment Committee to make certain entertainers or main speakers are not allergic to flowers. Find out any other special considerations dictated by health or family history. As odd as this detail seems, you don't want a teary-eyed, sneezing speaker or singer.

Neither do you want to give the speaker a souvenir bottle of champagne, if he or she cannot tolerate alcohol.

☐ Update Status Report.

Month Five

(Three months before major event)

☐ Check with facility and caterers to make certain of their needs for flowers or other decorations.

☐ Update Status Report.

Months Six-Seven

(One-two months before the event)

☐ Re-check to make certain all favors and souvenirs are on target for delivery.

☐ Re-check to make certain all centerpieces are on target for delivery. This point is particularly important, if you are having flowers flown in.

☐ Confer with Cleanup Chair to discuss what should be saved or disposed of after the event.

☐ Update Status Report.

One week before the event

☐ Stuff all favors/souvenirs into goody bags.

☐ Re-confirm delivery of centerpieces.

☐ Update Status Report.

Day of the event

☐ Allow extra time, because something will always go wrong.

☐ Work with facility and Arrangements/Logistics Chair in securing any large props for safety purpose.

☐ Work with Cleanup Chair to determine what should be saved or tossed away.

Month Eight

(Within two weeks after event)

☐ Complete post-event written report for Event Chair.

Months Nine-Ten

(One-two months after event)

☐ Take care of thank-you notes and calls.

☐ Submit suggestions for fine-tuning next year's event.

☐ Set up calendar for a new project.

Forms and Outlines

Status Report

Duplicate this form for each of your subchair people and for yourself. Use it to monitor each committee monthly, periodically, or at each committee meeting. Have the chair list the committee's responsibilities for that period, who is in charge of each, the deadline, budget, and status at the time of each report. After the event, you will have a running time line for the next event team to use in planning. Here is a sample report. The blank one follows.

Status Report
(refer to monthly calendar)

Chair Person: Decorating   Caroline Coons
Event: MS Costume Ball
Current Date: April 10, 2000
Event Date: October 10, 2000

Item	Responsible Person	Due Date	Status	Budget
Form Decorating Committee	Caroline Coons	4/30/00	All positions filled	-0-
Decide on tablecloths, napkins, flowers, and centerpieces designed around the theme of the event	Beth Erickson	4/15/00	Visited site, discussed theme and colors	
Meet with facility personnel on suggestions for your theme. They may have special contacts that may be helpful.	Caroline and Beth	5/1/00	Met with facility personnel	

Forms and Outlines *(continued)*

Status Report
(refer to monthly calendar)

Chair Person: Decorating
Event:
Current Date:
Event Date:

Item	Responsible Person	Due Date	Status	Budget

Entertainment and Auction Chair

Responsibilities

- Organize entertainment or music required for the event.
- Coordinate event auction, including acquisition and sale of items.

Qualifications

- Experienced organizer of entertainment at events.
- Knowledgeable about how to find entertainment.
- Experienced in organizing a charity auction.

Arranging Entertainment

Entertainment at an event can range in relative importance from soft, recorded music as guests arrive to a big-cast variety spectacular that is the highlight of the evening. It can range in professionalism from as simple as a Boy Scout troop that presents the colors up to a world-renowned figure you're paying mega-bucks, plus travel and hotel. Whatever the level or importance, however, entertainment that meets or exceeds expectations will enhance your event, and entertainment that falls on its face will produce embarrassment, grumbling, or worse. Of all the elements of the event, entertainment is the one probably most prone to have something go wrong. Your job is to plan, prepare, and foresee, to minimize the chances of a misfire.

The initial planning of the event normally will determine the kind and extent of entertainment needed. Be sure you don't focus so much on the major entertainment that you forget the incidental entertainment, such as strolling strings at the pre-dinner cocktail hour or playing a recording of the national anthem for the color guard.

If you are working closely with a charity organization, consult it first about "name" entertainment. An entertainer may be already associated with the particular charity you are supporting. If not, someone in the organization may recommend people who have worked well with other events.

If you do not secure entertainment through the charity organization, then you must find and audition entertainment or music. Audition any entertainment prior to making a final commitment. Ask for references from producers of other events similar to yours in style and venue where the entertainer has performed.

Match the entertainment to the style and size of your audience, as well as to your site. Entertainment that is terrific late at night in an intimate club could bomb with a tuxedo-and-gown audience in a large ballroom. If your potential entertainment is vocal, whether songs, commentary, or jokes, be certain that the content is appropriate for your audience. You may need to eliminate risqué lines or profanity.

Arrangements with entertainment should be in writing and signed. The contract should specify the following:

- What comprises the entertainment group. (You don't want to audition a full band and have a trio using the same name show up.)

- The time and length of the performance. (You don't want a twenty-minute segment to expand to an hour, or an expected hour to shrink to two fifteen-minute sets with a thirty-minute break in between.)

- Staging, setup, warm-up, equipment, piano, lighting, electrical, or other requirements of the entertainment that it is not providing itself.

- The fee, including when it is to be paid, such as half in advance, half after the performance, and to whom. (Should the check be made payable to a performer? Agent? Business name?)

- The extra charge if the entertainment is extended. (For example, the after-dinner dance is going great and you want to delay the band's wrap-up from 11:00 until midnight.)

- A penalty provision if the entertainment fails to show up.

Assign one person to handle the arrival, pickup, transportation, and so forth for entertainers coming in for the event, so there's no miscommunication among committee members.

If the entertainment is electronic (video, telecast, recorded music, etc.), arrange with the site and/or other vendors for the necessary content, equipment, and permissions, and for someone to operate whatever equipment is involved. Make sure the operator (not someone else) tests the equipment in advance. Make sure the operator has adequate lighting (even if a penlight) to see what he's doing. Nothing displays incompetence more than having some flustered person fiddling with equipment he can't run correctly.

Coordinate closely with these other chairs:

- Decorations and Donations chairs to be sure there are no conflicts in setup or other details between the entertainment, decorations, or exhibits.

- Public Relations Chair and the entertainers' publicist, if your entertainment is newsworthy in the context of your community, such as a Hollywood celebrity coming to a small city, or as a general-news or entertainment-news item, such as a well-known singer who makes the first stage appearance since battling cancer for a year.

- Cleanup Chair to arrange for the take-down and return of all equipment, staging, and other items associated with the entertainment that the entertainment is not handling itself.

Running an Auction

A live auction, silent auction, or both are key ingredients for many events, especially fund raisers held to benefit a school, church, or other organization staging the event. Auctions are great fund raisers, because donors can participate at a dollar level that is comfortable for them without embarrassment. One young couple can buy an autographed soccer ball for twenty dollars, while their daughter's classmate's parents fork over $5,000 for a packaged trip to Europe, and both couples have a good time. As a general principle, live auctions should be restricted to a small-to-moderate number of items projected to sell for hundreds or thousands of dollars. A silent auction should be used for numerous items projected to sell for anywhere from several dollars to the low hundreds.

There are three stages to running an auction:

1. Preparation and obtaining the auction items,

2. Conducting the auction, and

3. Handling the payment and delivery of the items sold or returning the items not sold.

Preparation and Obtaining Auction Items

- Line up a large, energetic, and detail-oriented committee, including a person qualified to be cashier.

- Prepare an auction-item receipt form that will be completed by the donor. The donor should provide on the auction-item receipt form the retail value and a description, directions, conditions, or whatever is appropriate for the item, and should be given an opportunity to specify a minimum acceptable price. Where the item donated is a service (for example, an architect's consultation) or the use of property (such as a week at a lakeside cabin), the donor should provide a letter that includes all of the relevant information, including any conditions or limitations, such as available dates, and a deadline for use, and the number of people permitted to use.

- Prepare auction-item solicitation instructions that will be used by everyone in your organization (not just your committee) in seeking auction items. Use your organization's newsletter or other means of communications to make sure everyone knows to seek items.

- Arrange for and coordinate with the auctioneer, if a live auction is taking place. Arrange for an introducer, if you are using a celebrity auctioneer.

- Coordinate the solicitation and pickup and delivery of donations.

- If you are having a live auction, combine items to create higher-price packages. For example, combine a pair of plane tickets donated by a travel agent with a week-long use of a distant resort facility. Or combine a restaurant dinner for four, tickets to a stage show, and the use of a limousine to create a luxury night on the town.

- Prepare a list with descriptions of auction items for the event program, including any minimum prices.

- Design, print, and fill out bid sheets for silent auction and information sheets for the auctioneer's use during a live auction. The bid sheet should include the minimum price and specify a minimum acceptable bid increment, to avoid "one-cent higher" bids.

Conducting the Auction

- Set up silent auction tables along walls or otherwise so they are accessible only from the front. The bid sheet should be securely fastened to the table in front of the item. Make sure there are plenty of inexpensive pens at the tables. Secure small items, to minimize the chances they will "walk away." Organize tables for the silent auction by category, for example:

  Day Trips and Getaways

  Services and Lessons

  Arts and Treasures

  Food and Restaurants

  Gift Baskets

  Sports and Celebrity Memorabilia

- Arrange the live-auction stage and microphone with the Arrangements and Logistics Chair, including a holding area for the items to be auctioned. The silent auction should be available for bidding as soon as the doors open to the event.

- Schedule when bidding on each table will close. A staggered schedule makes sure the cashier is not overwhelmed. Have a committee member assigned to take the bid sheets from the table exactly at the posted conclusion of the bidding. Be aware that bidding on popular items can be frantic at the deadline; in fairness to all bidders, the deadline should be observed, not extended.

- As soon as the sheets are picked up, the committee member should distinctively mark them to designate the winning bidder (such as by circling the winning name or drawing a line immediately beneath it with a red pen).

- After bidding has closed, take auction items to a central payment and pickup area that is secure from the sides and from behind. Be sure to keep items in order, so they can be located quickly.

- Unsold items can be consolidated at a "bargain table" for sale at a reduced rate.

- A committee member should assist the auctioneer during the live auction and should get the name of the successful bidder (or number, if bid paddles are used).

Receiving Money and Delivering Auction Items

You will receive money for items purchased at the auction. Provide a table at the pickup and payment location for a cashier and at least one assistant. The auction sheets should be taken to this table and arranged in alphabetical order by name of the winning bidder. As bidders arrive, the auction sheets should be checked to confirm that the correct person is claiming each item. Use a three-part receipt book to prepare a receipt for the buyer. Attach a copy of the receipt to the bidding sheet. An assistant should then get the item and give it to the buyer.

When accepting a check, be sure the check contains name, address, and telephone number, and that it is made payable to your organization, is signed and dated. If you wish to accept credit cards and the organization does not already have a merchant account, you will have to find a business (ideally, a member of your organization) that will allow you to use its account and will provide the necessary equipment and forms. Be sure to get written instructions on how to process credit payments. If you are accepting cash, be sure to have a cash box with sufficient currency and coins to make change. Check your state and local law to determine if you are required to collect sales tax. If so, make sure you know the procedure.

After sales are completed, tally all checks, credit card slips, and cash, and check the total against the total from the receipts written. Arrange with the organization treasurer for deposit of checks and cash. Arrange with the merchant-account person for processing the credit card slips, if not processed electronically at the event. The merchant account should receive the funds from the credit card company within about two to three days, and should then write a check to the organization for the amount of the credit card sales, less the credit card company's charge for processing, which will typically be about three percent. Of course you can ask if the merchant account holder will absorb this cost as an in-kind donation.

Collect unsold items for return to the donors, retention for sale at another time, or donation.

Calendar

Establishing Your Calendar

Many major events take a year to plan. For events with big-ticket auction items, a long lead time may be necessary, to deal with donors and their budget cycles. For either a yearlong campaign or a major event, complete groundwork listed in the calendar for Months One and Two at least six months before the event.

Many events can be pulled off with flair only a few months ahead of time. You may even put on an event Fast!—within a few weeks. Whether you plan to do a yearlong campaign, a mid-sized event, or a Fast! event, you must follow some basic steps. The following calendar contains the fundamental entertainment and auction checkpoints for almost any event, although the months may have to be condensed to fit your timetable.

Calendar Checklist for a Yearlong Campaign or Major Event

Month One

(Seven to ten months before major event)

❑ Form Entertainment and Auction Committee.

❑ Start thinking about a charity spokesperson and entertainers for the event. The spokesperson could come directly from the charity. Perhaps the charity has a connection with agents or celebrities.

❑ Update Status Report.

Month Two

(At least six months before major event)

❑ Finalize the participation of speakers and celebrities.

❑ Check out and finalize, if possible, musical performers. The Event Chair should sign all contracts.

❑ Update Status Report.

Month Three

(Five months before major event)

❑ Check with entertainment group liaison or agent for special needs, equipment, transportation, hotels, and dietary requirements.

❑ Gather promotional material regarding the entertainment. Give to Public Relations Chair for news releases and advertisement.

❑ If you are having a live auction, line up the auctioneer.

❑ Update Status Report.

Month Four

(Four months before major event)

❏ Follow up with entertainment group for any special requests.

❏ Coordinate the solicitation, pickup, and delivery of auction donations.

❏ Begin list with descriptions of auction items for programs, including minimum prices.

❏ Update Status Report.

Month Five

(Three months before major event)

❏ If you have a charity spokesperson, make sure arrangements have been made for travel, hotel, and meals for day of event. Coordinate with the Arrangements Chair.

❏ Step up solicitation of auction items.

❏ Update Status Report.

Month Six

(Two months before the event)

❏ Follow up with entertainment.

❏ Design and print bid sheets for silent auction and information sheets for the auctioneer's use during a live auction.

❏ Update Status Report.

Month Seven

(One month before the event)

❏ Confirm speaker and entertainment. Work with Event Chair and Arrangements Chair for a back-up speaker, in case an emergency prevents your first choice from appearing.

☐ Work with Public Relations Chair on the press release to give the entertainment adequate credit.

☐ Pinpoint and solicit auction items in categories that might need strengthening.

☐ Update Status Report.

One week before the event

☐ Follow up with entertainment.

☐ Help conduct a dress rehearsal of the event with the entertainers.

☐ Work with the Arrangements Chair to confirm that the staging guide is realistic: Double-check times and set time limits for speakers, entertainment, participants, and the core committee.

☐ Create a schedule that sets the time to close bidding on each auction table and defines who will pick up the bid sheets.

☐ Update Status Report.

Day of the event

☐ Allow extra time, because something will always go wrong.

☐ Provide transportation for dignitaries and guest speakers who need it.

☐ Make certain all necessary items are in place for the entertainers and speakers.

☐ If appropriate, make sure a special room is set aside for entertainers with convenient items, such as food and drink, restroom facilities, chairs, mirrors, and coat racks.

☐ After event, make sure entertainers have transportation to return to the airport, hotel, or wherever they are going.

❑ Set up silent auction tables and bid sheets. Work with Volunteers Committee and Arrangements Committee to make certain last-minute staffing is adequate.

❑ See that a committee member or more assist the auctioneer during the live auction.

❑ After bidding is closed, take auction items to a central payment and pickup area that is secure from the sides and from behind.

❑ Receive auction money and tally the totals.

❑ Collect unsold items.

Month Eight

(Within two weeks after the event)

❑ Complete post-event written report for Event Chair.

❑ Hold event team wrap-up meeting, while details of the event are fresh.

Month Nine

(One month after the event)

❑ Take care of thank-you notes and calls.

❑ Submit suggestions for fine-tuning next year's event.

Month Ten

(Two months after the event)

❑ Begin planning next event.

A Gala Event!

Forms and Outlines

Status Report

Duplicate this form for each of your subchair people and for yourself. Use it to monitor committee status monthly, periodically, or at each committee meeting. Have the chair list the committee's responsibilities for that period, who is in charge of each, the deadline, budget, and status at the time of each report. After the event, you will have a running time line for the next event team to use in planning. Here is a sample report. The blank one follows.

Status Report
(refer to monthly calendar)

Chair Person: Entertainment and Auction   Kitty Carlisle
Event: MS Costume Ball
Current Date: April 10, 2000
Event Date: October 10, 2000

Item	Responsible Person	Due Date	Status	Budget
Form Committee	Kitty Carlisle	4/30/00	All positions filled	-0-
Make list of potential celebrity guests	Don McKeon	4/15/00	Consulted charity office. They will contact their celebrity for us.	
Begin auction plans	Kitty & Jenny Billig	5/1/00	Event chair wants auction to go with baseball theme. Began plans for items to solicit.	

Forms and Outlines *(continued)*

Status Report
(refer to monthly calendar)

Chair Person: Entertainment and Auction
Event:
Current Date:
Event Date:

Item	Responsible Person	Due Date	Status	Budget

Bid Sheet

Bid Sheet

Item and #

Description of Item

Value of Item

(Raise bid in increments of _____)

Name or Number (which is assigned) of Person Bidding	Bid

Invitation and Program Chair

Responsibilities

- Oversee the design and printing of invitations, map, place cards, and associated materials.
- Secure advertising for, produce, and have printed the event program book or booklet.

Qualifications

- Experience with printers and designers.

Setting the Tone in Print

The invitations and other printed materials set the tone of your event. A cheap or sloppy invitation denotes a cheap or sloppy event. An elegant invitation promises an elegant event. The printed materials should harmonize with each other and portray the theme and style of the event. Your principal tasks are as follows:

- Design the invitations and any other printed materials, making sure all the pertinent information is included. Pertinent information on the invitation or program includes the type of event; when, where, and what time the event will be held; prices or suggested donations.

- Select an appropriate printer.

- Bring a design layout—a sample of what the invitation will actually look like—to the full committee meeting, so people will see exactly what it looks like. If a computer-generated or hand-drawn sample isn't feasible, at least bring the wording, along with samples of the paper and typeface.

- Work with the Event Chair and Donations Chair to develop donor categories, so guests can be recognized for donations that are more than the ticket price—whether or not they attend.

- Whenever feasible, list committee members somewhere on the invitations. Potential guests often like to know if prominent local personalities will be at the event, because they know them or wish to meet them for social or business reasons.

- Make sure the entire event team proofreads the invitation. The team should go through the copy carefully to make sure all the pertinent information is included. Make sure all the sponsors who want to be recognized on the program are included and their names are spelled correctly. Check and double-check. Is someone in your group a professional editor? If so, take advantage of the editor's expertise.

- See to it that all parties who need to look at the program and invitation do so and initial them.

- Make sure the invitations are printed on schedule, so they can be addressed and sent out on time.

- Use stamps on the invitations, whenever possible, not metered mail.

- Whenever possible, include personal notes from committee members in the appropriate invitations. For invitees you do not know personally, include a generic note from the chair, such as "Hope you will join us— Charity Jones, Chair."

Invitation Details

Your invitation should fit the occasion. You get only one chance to make a good first impression, and the invitation sets the tone for the event. The paper stock you select, the typeface you choose, the artwork and graphics, and the layout of the elements on the page join with the specifics about who, what, when, and where to give the recipient a good idea whether the event will be casual or formal, lively or stately. For an evening of jazz, you wouldn't send out invitations in the fancy script used for formal weddings.

Being invited to a party is fun. Your invitations should get people excited about coming to the event from the moment they open the envelope.

You might have someone on the committee who is a graphic artist who can help oversee the design of the invitation and program, but if possible, have the pieces produced professionally. You'll save time and expense in the long run. Some designers offer a price break to nonprofit organizations.

As you develop your invitation, keep these points in mind:

- Consider choosing one of many preprinted papers available to use.

- Most printers can be helpful in advising you about the mood that typefaces engender, although a professional designer will know and make choices accordingly.

- Often printers will help you select a layout as well.

- Pertinent information on the invitation includes what type of event it is; when, where, and what time the event will be held; the name of the charity; prices or suggested donations; and how to respond.

- Include a postage-paid response envelope and a response card for a significantly higher R.s.v.p. and contribution rate. Consider including a donation check-off on the response card, making it convenient for people to contribute, even if they can't attend the event.

- The entire event team should look over the invitation before it is printed to make sure everything is included and there are no errors. Be aware that headline type—the most important—is often overlooked by proofreaders who are not professionals. Double-check all headlines.

- Ask the printer to donate or discount his services in return for acknowledgment in the program. Don't forget to give the donating or discounting printer a complimentary pair of tickets to the event.

- Mail the invitations early. If you are conducting a year-long campaign, mail them two months ahead of time. Otherwise, count on three to four weeks. Use stamps—not a metered stamp.

- One way that your company can maximize its contact is by printing a list of short facts about the company or cause on a detachable flap on the donation envelope.

- Take a complete invitation to the post office and weigh it, to make sure you'll have the right amount of postage on each.

Addressing Invitations

Invitations to a formal event should be addressed as carefully as those for a wedding. You'll need a committee to help. Each member should have excellent handwriting and be attentive to detail. Here are the rules for formal invitations:

- Spell out symbols (such as "and" instead of using an ampersand).
- Write out the full name.
- The only abbreviations allowed are Dr., Mr., Mrs., Ms, and Jr.
- No middle initials are allowed; spell out the name. If you don't know what the initial stands for, omit it.
- Never write "and family."
- Write out "East," "West," "North," and "South."
- Only house numbers and the ZIP code may be written as numerals; spell out everything else as a word ("Twenty-fifth Avenue" instead of "25th Avenue").
- Write out "Avenue" and similar words (such as "Road" and "Street").
- Spell out the name of the state.
- Use permanent black ink.
- Fountain pens or felt-tip pens with medium or wide points are best for hand-addressing invitations. Use a calligrapher if possible

Program Details

The program is the book or booklet distributed to each attendee at the event. It can range from a simple 8½" x 11" sheet folded in half up to a 200-page slick paper magazine. The program sets a tone for the event, as does the invitation. The program can be a key fund-raising instrument through the sale of advertising. It also is a principal means of giving the sponsors and committee members due credit and their "place in the sun."

Your initial task is deciding the style and size of the program, and whether it will include advertising. If your event includes an auction, then the program will include the list of auction items. If your event is annual, or you want to keep your organization or charity visible to event guests, consider a "weighty" book-like program they are likely to keep.

Program advertising has a wide range. A small pamphlet-size program may include a couple of "courtesy" ads from the businesses of organization members that donated money or services to pay for its printing. A large program may have numerous pages of ads sold as a fund-raising technique.

If you undertake a serious advertising effort, appoint an Advertising and Layout Subcommittee Chair, because there will be substantial work to do.

Tasks to produce the program include these:

- Decide the format and design of the program. Consult with your printer in setting page size and number of pages, so you don't inadvertently run the printing cost up by using nonstandard configurations. Keep the type font legible. Make certain attendees can read the auction items listed. Don't forget that overhead lighting may be dimmed during the event. The event may even be candlelit.

- Make sure the computer software used in producing the program is compatible with the printer and others you must work with on this project.

- Establish rates for advertising. Seek full-page ads and make them your best space-for-dollar buy, but also provide for half-page, quarter-page, and business-card ads. For example, if you charge $250 for a full page, make a half-page $150, a quarter-page $100, and a business card $50. Charge a premium for back cover, inside front, and inside back covers.

- Establish a calendar of deadlines for advertising, copy, and delivery of material to printer.

- Work with one printer to determine if you can get a better price for all the printing needs if combined.

- Enter into the computer all the committee chairs, honorary chairs, sponsors, event program, and other information critical for a successful program book. Update early and often.

- Work closely with volunteers and others who may know potential advertisers such as shopkeepers, doctors, hairdressers, restaurants, auto dealerships, amusement parks, etc.

- Design and produce a one-page solicitation letter to send to potential advertisers.

- Design and produce a one-page specification and rate sheet for advertisers.

- Design and produce a one-page Advertisement Order Form that includes the advertiser's contact points, size of ad, and other relevant information.

- Have numerous volunteers and committee members contact businesses and philanthropic organizations by phone, fax, e-mail, or personal visits to solicit ads.

- Assist advertisers in designing ads for program (if needed).

- Design advertisement for Internet links with other Web sites (if needed).

- Pick up copy and checks from advertisers if not received by mail. Arrange with organization treasurer for deposit of funds.

- Work with the Event Chair and Public Relations Chair to make sure all relevant editorial copy is available and

included in the program, if it is a large program book.
Information may include articles about the benefiting
charity, lead sponsor, and history of the event; pictures
of key leaders, speakers, or entertainers; lists of sponsors, donors, volunteers, and committees; and the program schedule. Also include an index of advertisers.
That list provides an extra mention, and makes it easy
for advertisers to find their ad.

- You must very carefully read the "blue line" proof the
printer will give you prior to printing the program. If
you have provided the printer with camera-ready copy
for the program, the main thing to check on the blue
line is that pages have not gotten out of order, been
dropped, or duplicated. If photographs are included in
the program, make sure each photo has been placed in
the correct spot, so that, for example, the charity's pres-
ident isn't misidentified as the singer. Make sure photographs are cropped and sized as intended.

- Arrange for delivery of the printed programs. If you are
producing large program books, they will take a great
deal of space—for example, a thousand 200-page books
could fill about thirty cartons. You must coordinate with
the Arrangements Chair, to arrange a place to deliver
the books that will minimize handling, once they are
delivered.

A Gala Event!

Calendar

Establishing Your Calendar

Many major events can take a year to plan. For either a yearlong campaign or a major event, complete the groundwork listed in the calendar for Months One and Two at least six months before the event.

Many events can be pulled off with flair only a few months ahead of time. You may even put on an event Fast!—within a few weeks. Whether you plan to do a yearlong campaign, a mid-sized event, or a Fast! event, you must follow some basic steps. The following calendar contains the fundamental invitation and program checkpoints for almost any event, although the months may have to be condensed to fit your timetable.

Calendar Checklist for a Yearlong Campaign or Major Event

Month One

(Seven to ten months before major event)

❑ Form your committee.

❑ Begin planning how the format of the invitation and program should fit the event theme.

❑ Update Status Report.

Month Two

(At least six months before major event)

❑ Finalize everybody for your committee.

❑ Determine if your committee can design the invitation and program or whether you must go to an outside design vendor.

❏ Contact printer for cost of printing invitations and program. Check to be sure the computer software used by your committee is compatible with the printer's software, especially if you want to design your own printed material to save money.

❏ Begin designing a rate sheet for potential advertisers.

❏ Refine mailing and invitation lists. Work closely with Mailing List Chair.

❏ Update Status Report.

Month Three

(Five months before major event)

❏ Write and design the invitation. Be sure to include all necessary information and clear directions.

❏ Update Status Report.

Month Four

(Four months before major event)

❏ Order invitations. Proof invitations carefully! Have several proofreaders; each should initial the proof.

❏ Update Status Report.

Month Five

(Three months before major event)

❏ Send advance invitations to sponsors and underwriters.

❏ Send invitations to prominent people.

❏ Help finalize invitation mailing list.

❏ Contact a calligrapher. Perhaps there are members on the committee who do calligraphy.

❏ Update Status Report.

Month Six

(Two months before the event)

❑ Prepare to mail invitations four to six weeks before your event, if it is a massive one; otherwise, wait until three or four weeks in advance.

❑ Schedule a gathering of committee members to address invitations.

❑ Have committee members write personal notes to include with or on the invitation.

❑ Make sure only a stamp is used on envelope. (Do not use metered stamps.)

❑ Immediately follow up on the invitations sent to "key" invitees to ask for their commitment to attend your event.

❑ Collect information from Auction Chair on items to be listed in program.

❑ Make sure the program format and advertising is developing.

❑ Update Status Report.

Month Seven

(One month before the event)

❑ As invitations are mailed and responses received, follow up with phone calls. By calling, you make sure the invitation was received and that all the information about the event is clear.

❑ Collect information from Auction Chair on items to be listed in program.

❑ Prepare a printed program.

❑ Update Status Report.

One week before the event

- ☐ Review and update R.s.v.p. list daily.
- ☐ Check for last-minute sponsors or insert material needed.
- ☐ Finalize the program and have it printed, if not already done.
- ☐ Prepare a step-by-step agenda for the big day. Include *all* pertinent information on this staging guide.
- ☐ Pick up printed programs from printer.
- ☐ Prepare tent cards for seating.
- ☐ Work with Event Chair and other chairs on a seating chart.
- ☐ Update Status Report.

Day of the event

- ☐ Make certain the check-in tables have multiple copies of guest lists and other necessary information.
- ☐ Distribute the programs to guests (placed at tables or given out at arrival).
- ☐ Have copies of your guest list available for future uses.

Month Eight

(Within two weeks after the event)

- ☐ Complete post-event written report for Event Chair.
- ☐ Follow up immediately with donors and key event participants.
- ☐ Hold event team wrap-up meeting, while details of the event are fresh.

Month Nine

(One month after the event)

- ❏ Take care of thank-you notes and calls.
- ❏ Critique the event.
- ❏ Begin planning next event.

Month Ten

(Two months after the event)

- ❏ Set up the calendar for a new project.

Forms and Outlines

Status Report

Duplicate this form for each of your subchair people and for yourself. Use it to monitor committee status monthly, periodically, or at each committee meeting. Have the chair list the committee's responsibilities for that period, who is in charge of each, the deadline, budget, and status at the time of each report. After the event, you will have a running time line for the next event team to use in planning. Here is a sample report. The blank one follows.

Status Report
(refer to monthly calendar)

Chair Person: Invitation and Program   Amelia Earhart
Event: MS Costume Ball
Current Date: April 10, 2000
Event Date: October 10, 2000

Item	Responsible Person	Due Date	Status	Budget
Form Committee	Amelia Earhart	4/30/00	All positions filled	-0-
Begin talks with artists re: baseball theme for invitations	Julie Mackie	4/15/00	Met with designer and printer to decide affordable format	
Start gathering names for invitation addressers	Vickie Tolar	5/1/00	Announcement made at annual meeting	

Status Report
(refer to monthly calendar)

Chair Person: Invitation and Program
Event:
Current Date:
Event Date:

Item	Responsible Person	Due Date	Status	Budget

Forms and Outlines *(continued)*

Sample Invitation

Simple Simon Pie Company

cordially invites you to attend

The Leader Dogs for the Blind

Gala Dinner

The Holly Hills Wood Hotel

6000 North Hudson Place

Washington, Virginia

Grand Ballroom

Thursday Evening, May 3, 0000

Reception 6:00 p.m.

Dinner 7:00 p.m.

Black Tie

R.sv.p. by [Date]
[Telephone number]

Sample R.s.v.p. Card (front)

Simple Simon Pie Company / Leader Dogs for the Blind

(return address)

Yes...I would like to attend the Leader Dogs for the Blind Black Tie Dinner

_____ Please reserve _____ tables of 10 at $1,000 per table.

_____ Please reserve _____ places at $100 per person.

_____ Enclosed is a check in the amount of $_____ .

Sorry, I cannot attend the dinner; however, I still wish to make a contribution in recognition of the charity in the amount of $_____ .

Name _____

Address _____

Phone (Business)_____ ____ (Home) _____

E-Mail_____

Checks should be made payable to Leader Dogs for the Blind and are tax deductible to the extent of the law.

Please list the names of guests covered by this reservation on the reverse side.

Forms and Outlines *(continued)*

Sample R.s.v.p. Card (back)

Attendee Names

_____

_____

_____

_____

_____

_____

_____

_____

_____

_____

_____

_____

_____

_____

_____

_____

_____

Mailing List Chair

Responsibilities

- Compile the contact mailing list and keep it current.

Qualifications

- Proficient in using a computer and a database program such as Microsoft Access or FileMaker Pro.

Gathering and Maintaining the Mailing List

The quality of the mailing list compiled for the event will determine how successful an event your group can produce. The mailing list is the principal tool that the Invitations and Donations Chairs will use in generating attendance and contributions to the event.

Begin with a basic membership or other list. Obtain additions to the list from other committee members and from the contacts made by other committee chairs. Work closely with other committee chairs to incorporate all the lists from everyone on the committee and from the national or regional charity. One way to expand the mailing list quickly is to ask each member on the mailing list committee—or the entire event team— to contribute 30 to 50 names.

Also be alert for names or lists that may be available outside your organization, such as from friends, local businesses, and trade organizations. If your event is large or you are appealing to a geographically broad audience, you may want to consider purchasing a mailing list from a commercial mailing-list broker.

Be aware, however, that the more remote the names on the list are from your organization, your charity, or your locale, the lower your acceptance or contribution rate will be. Don't waste money on printing and mailing to names highly unlikely to respond.

Your mailing list should be maintained in a computerized database. Attempting to operate without a computer from a series of photocopied sheets or handwritten index card lists will be inefficient, frustrating, and error-creating.

Establish your database file with the following fields for each name or record. Not all may be available or needed in each case, but if you set up the form completely at the outset, it will be easy to sort and add information as time goes on.

- Honorific (e.g., Mr., Mrs., Mr. & Mrs., Ms, The Hon., Dr., The Rev.)
- First name
- Middle name
- Last name (dividing the name into separate data fields facilitates alphabetizing the list)
- Business title
- Organization

- Address line 1
- Address line 2
- City
- State
- Zip
- Home telephone
- Business telephone
- Fax number
- Cellular telephone
- E-mail address
- Web site address (for businesses and other organizations)
- Source of name (mailing list or other source of name)
- Additional fields as appropriate to your event to categorize names, record follow-up, etc.

Check for and delete duplicates periodically as the list is compiled. To check for duplicates, sort the entire list by last name, then first name, then address, and duplicates will be sorted next to each other. When planning for your event takes several months, be alert for changes in information.

Once compiled, your list can be used to generate an event mailing list for mailing labels, printed envelopes, or for persons hand-writing invitation envelopes. The same list also provides a telephone follow-up list, an R.s.v.p. checklist, name tags, place cards, and so forth. When you use a database, you can print all the information or only the information relevant to a particular need. Finally, of course, you have the list as your starting point for next year's event, complete with information on who did and did not respond.

Calendar

Establishing Your Calendar

Many major events take a year to plan. For either a year-long campaign or a major event, complete the groundwork listed in the calendar for Months One and Two at least six months before the event.

Many events can be pulled off with flair only a few months ahead of time. You may even put on an event Fast!—within a few weeks. Whether you plan to do a yearlong campaign, a mid-sized event, or a Fast! event, you must follow some basic steps. The following calendar contains the fundamental mailing list checkpoints for almost any event, although the months may have to be condensed to fit your timetable.

Calendar Checklist for a Yearlong Campaign or Major Event

Month One

(Seven to ten months before major event)

- ☐ Form your committee. You or somebody on this committee will need to have good computer know-how.
- ☐ Determine the computer software to use and the information you will be collecting.
- ☐ Determine your target audience and begin to create a mailing list.
- ☐ Gather the names, addresses, phone and fax numbers, and e-mail or Web site addresses of helpful local business and community leaders.
- ☐ Update Status Report.

Month Two

(At least six months before major event)

❏ Have all committee members submit their lists.

❏ Refine mailing and invitation lists.

❏ Update Status Report.

Month Three

(Five months before major event)

❏ Refine and expand mailing list. Remind committee members to come up with names.

❏ Update Status Report.

Month Four

(Four months before major event)

❏ Further add to mailing lists.

❏ Update Status Report.

Month Five

(Three months before major event)

❏ Give mailing list to Invitation Chair to begin addressing.

❏ Update Status Report.

Month Six

(Two months before the event)

❏ Prepare to mail invitations four to six weeks before your event, if it is a massive one. Otherwise, wait until three or four weeks in advance. Be sure to order enough stamps for mailing. Work closely with Invitation Chair.

❏ Update Status Report.

Month Seven

(One month before the event)

❏ As invitations are mailed and responses received, follow up with phone calls. By calling, you make sure the invitation was received and that all the information about the event is clear. Work closely with Invitation Chair.

❏ Update Status Report.

One week before the event

❏ Review and update R.s.v.p. list daily.

❏ Update Status Report.

Day of the event

❏ Have copies of the guest list available for future uses. Work closely with Invitation Chair.

❏ Print name tags or place cards, if appropriate for event.

Month Eight

(Within two weeks after the event)

❏ Complete post-event written report for Event Chair.

❏ Hold event team wrap-up meeting, while details of the event are fresh.

Month Nine

(One month after the event)

- [ ] Take care of thank-you notes and calls.
- [ ] Critique the event.
- [ ] Clean up mailing list with returned invitations and non-responders.
- [ ] Give list on a computer disk to Event Chair, along with hard (printed) copies.

Month Ten

(Two months after the event)

- [ ] Set up the calendar for a new project.

Forms and Outlines

Status Report

Duplicate this form for each of your subchair people and for yourself. Use it to monitor committee status monthly, periodically, or at each committee meeting. Have the chair list the committee's responsibilities for that period, who is in charge of each, the deadline, budget, and status at the time of each report. After the event, you will have a running time line for the next event team to use in planning. Here is a sample report. The blank one follows.

Status Report
(refer to monthly calendar)

Chair Person: Mailing List   Ellen Banker
Event: MS Costume Ball
Current Date: April 10, 2000
Event Date: October 10, 2000

Item	Responsible Person	Due Date	Status	Budget
Form Committee	Ellen Banker	4/30/00	All positions filled	-0-
Determine the computer software to use and the information you will be collecting	Ellen	4/15/00	Bought most up-to-date version of Microsoft Access	$200.00
Determine target audience and begin to create a mailing list	Ellen, Bill Griffin	5/1/00	Met with event chair and charity liaison. Membership lists available from both. Brainstormed other lists	
Gather the names, addresses, phone and fax numbers, and e-mail or Web addresses of helpful local business and community leaders	Bill Griffin	5/30/00	Chamber of Commerce and local real estate group interested	

Status Report
(refer to monthly calendar)

Chair Person: Mailing List
Event:
Current Date:
Event Date:

Item	Responsible Person	Due Date	Status	Budget

Telephone Solicitation Chair

Responsibilities

- Organize the follow-up phone contacts to targeted supporters to ensure invitations have been received and are being considered.

Qualifications

- Good organizer.
- Comfortable speaking on telephone.

The Follow-Up

- Recruit a large committee to share the workload.
- Organize the mailing list into A, B, and C donors, if the list is large.
- Give committee members a list of names and numbers, along with a phone script.

- Work closely with the people mailing the invitations. A week after invitations are mailed, phones should begin ringing.

- For the best response, make sure top donors are contacted by committee members who know them. Emphasize how important these people are to the endeavor. If the invitees can't attend, be sure volunteers ask them if they would support a corporate table or make a donation.

- Three weeks before the event, committee members should call invitees again, if they have not responded.

- After the event, prominent invitees should receive a final phone call, whether they attended or donated. If they made a pledge, they should be thanked and reminded to put the event on their calendar for next year. If they didn't come, the caller should say something like, "We're so sorry you weren't able to attend, but we hope you'll put us on your calendar for next year."

- Give people on this committee specific guidelines and directions to help them in their calls. Ten is a reasonable number of people to expect each committee member to call. Try to make sure no one gets overlapping lists; you don't want two people calling the same invitee.

- Be pleasant, positive, and enthusiastic when calling guests and major contributors. Know how to give accurate but inspiring information about your cause.

A Gala Event!

Calendar

Establishing Your Calendar

Many major events take a year to plan. For either a year-long campaign or a major event, complete the groundwork listed in the calendar for Months One and Two at least six months before the event.

Many events can be pulled off with flair only a few months ahead of time. You may even put on an event Fast!—within a few weeks. Whether you plan to do a yearlong campaign, a mid-sized event, or a Fast! event, you must follow some basic steps. The following calendar contains the fundamental telephone follow-up checkpoints for almost any event, although the months may have to be condensed to fit your timetable.

Calendar Checklist for a Yearlong Campaign or Major Event

Month One

(Seven to ten months before major event)

❏ Form a large committee.
❏ Update Status Report.

Month Two

(At least six months before major event)

❏ Get lists from other chairs who might need to have calls made for them.
❏ Update Status Report.

Month Three

(Five months before major event)

❏ Write your sample phone-call script.

❏ Update Status Report.

Month Four

(Four months before major event)

❏ Give people on this committee specific guidelines and directions to help them in their calls.

❏ Update Status Report.

Month Five

(Three months before major event)

❏ Make phone calls when needed.

❏ Update Status Report.

Month Six

(Two months before the event)

❏ Make phone calls when needed.

❏ Update Status Report.

Month Seven

(One month before the event)

❏ Three weeks before the event, invitees should be called again, if they have not responded.

❏ Update Status Report.

One week before the event

☐ Make last-minute phone calls where appropriate.

☐ Update Status Report.

Day of the event

☐ Circulate among guests and donors to thank them for their contributions.

Month Eight

(Within two weeks after the event)

☐ Complete post-event written report for Event Chair.

☐ After the event, prominent invitees should receive a final phone call, whether they attended or donated.

☐ Hold event team wrap-up meeting, while details of the event are fresh.

Month Nine

(One month after the event)

☐ Take care of thank-you notes and calls.

☐ Critique the event.

Month Ten

(Two months after the event)

☐ Set up the calendar for a new project.

Forms and Outlines

Status Report

Duplicate this form for each of your subchair people and for yourself. Use it to monitor committee status monthly, periodically, or at each committee meeting. Have the chair list the committee's responsibilities for that period, who is in charge of each, the deadline, budget, and status at the time of each report. After the event, you will have a running time line for the next event team to use in planning. Here is a sample report. The blank one follows.

Status Report
(refer to monthly calendar)

Chair Person: Telephone Solicitation   Sarah Boyer
Event: MS Costume Ball
Current Date: April 10, 2000
Event Date: October 10, 2000

Item	Responsible Person	Due Date	Status	Budget
Form Committee	Sarah Boyer	4/10/00	All positions filled	-0-
Begin preparation of telephone scripts, including information on charity	Ann Gellman	4/15/00	Called charity for information guidelines to be included in script	

Status Report
(refer to monthly calendar)

Chair Person: Telephone Solicitation
Event:
Current Date:
Event Date:

Item	Responsible Person	Due Date	Status	Budget

Forms and Outlines *(continued)*

Sample Phone Script Invitation Follow-Up

Charity Caller: "Hello, may I speak with Mr./Ms. _____ please?"

"Mr./Ms. _____ , my name is _____ , and I am with _____ . I am calling to follow up on the _____ invitation you recently received. Do you plan to attend?"

(For positive response)

Mr. (Responder): Yes!

Charity Caller: "That's wonderful, Mr./Ms._____. I'm sure you agree that this is a worthwhile cause, and I look forward to meeting you. I will be looking for your R.s.v.p. card in the mail. If you know of anyone else who would be interested in participating or making a contribution, please have him or her contact me at (000) 000-0000. Goodbye."

(For negative response)

Mr. (Responder): No.

Charity Caller: "Well, it's a shame you won't be able to attend our charity event. Would there be anyone else in your family or company who you might send on your behalf?" (Response may be yes or no.)

(If yes . . .)

Charity Caller: "That's wonderful. I will look for your R.s.v.p. with their names. We're sorry you won't be able to join us, but please keep our event in mind for next year. Goodbye."

(If no . . .)

Charity Caller: "If you should change your mind or know of anyone who would care to participate, please call me at (000) 000-0000. I appreciate your taking the time to talk with me. Please keep our event in mind for next year. Goodbye."

Reservation Chair

Responsibilities

- Receives and compiles all responses and money sent in response to the invitations.
- Plans the seating charts and is responsible for the place cards for seating.

Qualifications

- Knowledge of spreadsheet software program.
- Good organizer.
- Experience with seating charts.

Taking the Calls

The reservations system is critical to the success of the event. Nothing will turn off guests quicker than showing up and finding their names are not on the reservation list, even though they called. Equally important, nothing will throw off logistics and budgets faster than a major overrun or underrun of guests as the result of a faulty reservations system. You, like the Mailing List Chair, should have an up-to-date and compatible spreadsheet program on your computer so you can electronically receive the invitation mailing list and record responses on it.

The first task is to determine what phone line will be used (or installed) to receive R.s.v.p. calls. The line should be dedicated to the event, so that (1) callers won't get a busy signal because of other personal or business use of the line; (2) anyone answering the phone will do so in the name of the event; and (3) an answering machine can respond in the name of the event, not in some generic way that leaves callers wondering if they reached the right phone number. If most respondents will be local, make sure to use a phone number that is local. As soon as the number is determined, provide it to the Invitation Chair for placement on invitations.

If the R.s.v.p. process also includes receiving payment for tickets, provide an R.s.v.p. address for persons who wish to pay by check. This address will usually be your organization's, although you may want to consider a separate box address, if you expect a large volume of mail responses or if you want to be sure that R.s.v.p. notes don't get lost amid a heavy volume of regular mail for the organization.

Shortly before invitations are mailed, obtain the mailing list in electronic form from the Mailing List Chair and set up your computerized system for recording R.s.v.p. information. This list should include name, whether or not the caller is coming, number of persons in the party, any special requests (for example, vegetarian dinner, wheelchair seating, seat next to Mr. & Mrs. Jones, etc.), and ticketing and payment information as is appropriate to the event.

When invitations are mailed, record an event message on the R.s.v.p. phone equipment that tells respondents what information to leave if the phone is not answered personally (name and phone number of caller, whether coming to event, number of persons in the party, special requests, payment information as appropriate). Be sure someone checks the message machine frequently, so it doesn't overflow and so the database is kept current. If you are getting responses by mail, be sure the mail repository is checked daily. Credit-card information must be promptly relayed to the person processing credit-card payments.

Keep the Event Chair advised of the running count of acceptances and declines. Provide the Telephone Chair with regular updates of who has responded, so non-responders can be called and responders will not be called. Daily or even twice-daily updates will be needed beginning one week prior to the event, including one as close as possible to the time at which the food service guarantee must be made.

Seating the Guests

Develop the event seating chart, if needed. This delicate task must be done in coordination with the Event Chair, Charity Liaison Chair, Invitation Chair, and other key Event Committee members. The seating chart should be kept on a computer, so it can be changed easily, which will happen with great regularity, until the guests are actually seated. Some of the considerations for seating include the following:

- If there is a head table, begin with the people who must be seated there.
- Identify people who need particularly good seats—major donors, principal officials of the charity you're supporting, and so on. If the chair has any doubts or questions about who should sit with whom, he or she should ask the Charity Liaison Chair for guidance.
- Try to accommodate requests of guests to be seated with other guests.

- If diplomatic or government officials will be attending, be certain to adhere to the requirements of protocol. If you are uncertain, call the U.S. State Department Protocol Office for assistance with diplomatic seating or the relevant federal, state, or local office.
- Be alert to people who should not be seated with each other for any known reasons.
- Try to avoid overloading tables with men or women.
- Identify seating for persons with disabilities.

Number the tables and arrange with the Logistics Chair for numbers to be placed on the tables where people can see them when looking for their table. For a very large event, either prepare a large diagram of the numbered tables and hang it by the entrance to the room or have a hostess assisting guests with seating.

Set out place cards if they are being used, put table numbers on tickets, or put table numbers on the guest lists at a reception table.

Coordinate and supervise ushers or greeters. If guests must check in at a reception table, prepare guest lists for the table staff to use, and arrange for that staff. Arrange for name tags, if they are to be used. Do not use name tags at formal events.

If some tickets are being picked up and paid for at the event, arrange for a cashier. Make sure your controls are sufficient to ensure that everyone who should pay does so.

As guests are taking their seats, be sure you are readily available to resolve seating confusions quickly. At every event, a few people will decide to sit with their friends, regardless of the table assignments. You will need to make quick adjustments to accommodate those changes.

If seating is open, or if persons with reservations do not show, try to consolidate partial tables, so you don't have two people at one table, two at another, four at a third, and so forth, when most tables seat six at that event.

If name tags are displayed on registration table, someone should gather them up once the program begins to avoid guests perusing the names of no-shows.

Calendar

Establishing Your Calendar

Many major events take a year to plan. For either a yearlong campaign or a major event, complete the groundwork listed in the calendar for Months One and Two at least six months before the event.

Many events can be pulled off with flair only a few months ahead of time. You may even put on an event Fast!—within a few weeks. Whether you plan to do a yearlong campaign, a mid-sized event, or a Fast! event, you must follow some basic steps. The following calendar contains the fundamental reservations and seating checkpoints for almost any event, although the months may have to be condensed to fit your timetable.

Calendar Checklist for a Yearlong Campaign or Major Event

Month One

(Seven to ten months before major event)

❑ Form your committee. Work closely with the Invitation Chair.

❑ Update Status Report.

Month Two

(At least six months before major event)

❑ Help refine mailing and invitation lists.

❑ Update Status Report.

Month Three

(Five months before major event)

- [ ] Set up telephone lines for R.s.v.p. calls.
- [ ] Record message on phone lines for off-hours.
- [ ] Set up banking account or accounting procedure for accepting money.
- [ ] Help refine mailing list.
- [ ] Update Status Report.

Month Four

(Four months before major event)

- [ ] Update Status Report.

Month Five

(Three months before major event)

- [ ] Help finalize invitation and mailing list.
- [ ] Shortly before invitations are mailed, obtain mailing list from Mailing List Chair and set up computerized system for recording R.s.v.p. information.
- [ ] Update Status Report.

Month Six

(Two months before the event)

- [ ] Immediately follow up on the invitations sent to "key" invitees to ask for their commitment to attend your event.
- [ ] Update Status Report.

Month Seven

(One month before the event)

❑ As invitations are mailed and responses received, follow up with phone calls to key guests who haven't responded. By calling, you make sure the invitation was received and that all the information about the event is clear. Be sure to coordinate your calls with the Telephone Chair.

❑ Work with other chairs to develop a seating chart for event.

❑ Update Status Report.

One week before the event

❑ Review and update R.s.v.p. list daily.

❑ Update Status Report.

Day of the event

❑ Arrive early.

❑ Have copies of your guest list and seating chart available for future uses.

❑ Be on hand to troubleshoot.

❑ Gather up name tags of no-shows from registration table and put them away.

Month Eight

(Within two weeks after the event)

❑ Complete post-event written report for Event Chair.

❑ Hold event team wrap-up meeting, while details of the event are fresh.

Month Nine

(One month after the event)

- ☐ Take care of thank-you notes and calls.
- ☐ Critique the event.
- ☐ Begin planning next event.

Month Ten

(Two months after the event)

- ☐ Set up the calendar for a new project.

Forms and Outlines

Status Report

Duplicate this form for each of your subchair people and for yourself. Use it to monitor committee status monthly, periodically, or at each committee meeting. Have the chair list the committee's responsibilities for that period, who is in charge of each, the deadline, budget, and status at the time of each report. After the event, you will have a running time line for the next event team to use in planning. Here is a sample report. The blank one follows.

Status Report
(refer to monthly calendar)

Chair Person: Reservation   Noemi Taylor
Event: MS Costume Ball
Current Date: April 10, 2000
Event Date: October 10, 2000

Item	Responsible Person	Due Date	Status	Budget
Set up telephone lines for R.s.v.p. calls	Noemi Taylor	4/30/00	Phone company to install by 4/15	-0-
Record message on phone lines for off-hours	Noemi	4/15/00	Arranged for voice mail message to be read by event chair	
Set up banking account or accounting procedure for accepting money	Noemi	5/1/00	First National temporary account effective 5/1	
Help refine mailing list	Noemi, Mailing List Chair	5/30/00	Meeting 4/29 to review list	

Forms and Outlines *(continued)*

Status Report
(refer to monthly calendar)

Chair Person: Reservation
Event:
Current Date:
Event Date:

Item	Responsible Person	Due Date	Status	Budget

Volunteers Chair

Responsibilities

- Recruit and assign volunteers.
- Manage volunteers on all projects.

Qualifications

- Know a lot of people.
- Experience in managing large numbers of volunteers.

Finding and Using Volunteers

The committee chairs and the key assistants they recruit will be involved with the event from start to finish. In addition, numerous other volunteers may be needed for short-term, labor-intensive projects, such as addressing envelopes, stuffing goody bags, or staffing a reception table. The Volunteers Chair must recruit this pool of helpers and match availability and particular skills with the tasks and timetables set by the committee chairs. In effect, you are running a temporary-help agency.

To make best use of the volunteers and to staff all the needs, you must document all offers and requests.

- Design a Volunteer Task Form for committee chairs to use in requesting help. This form should include blanks for specifying the task, qualifications to perform the task, when it is to be performed, and how many volunteers are needed. Distribute copies of this form to committee chairs at the outset of planning.

- Design a Volunteer Availability Form (p. 176) that can be filled out by volunteers or by you or an assistant who is calling people to get them to volunteer. This form should include the volunteer's name, address, phone, e-mail, special skills (for example, professional designer; computer proficient), and general times of availability. Distribute copies of this form to all members of your organization at the outset of planning for the event.

- Set up a computerized database to record tasks and availability as forms come in from chairs and volunteers. Match tasks to volunteers as quickly as possible, and notify each party, preferably in writing.

You will have to recruit volunteers aggressively. Even people who are willing to work typically must be asked or reminded to sign up.

- Put notices in your organization newsletter, post fliers on its bulletin board, or use whatever means of communication available to seek volunteers.

- If your event is one that can appropriately use community volunteers, put notices in community newspapers, on community Web sites, or wherever else feasible.

- Call members of the organization who are not yet on a committee or in the volunteer database and seek their services. Remember that chairs will directly recruit volunteers, as well, from their personal contacts. Try to include these names, too, in your database, so that you don't waste time calling people who already have volunteered.

Stay in regular contact with committee chairs to be sure their needs are met, or to shift their excess volunteers to other tasks.

Work with your own contacts or with the Donations Chair to come up with small rewards for volunteers, especially those with onerous tasks. For example, you might pass out coffee-bar or fast-food gift certificates to volunteers who stick it out through a long afternoon of addressing envelopes.

After the event, send thank-you notes to the volunteers. If the volunteers work in groups, consider taking snapshots of the groups and sending a copy to each person with a simple message on the back.

Organize your final list of volunteers by tasks and jobs accomplished. Keep the list available for you or next year's Volunteers Chair to use as a starting point. Check with the committee chairs for recommendations on what volunteers would be good (or not good) to approach to be a chair next year.

A Gala Event!

Calendar

Establishing Your Calendar

Many major events take a year to plan. For either a year-long campaign or a major event, complete the groundwork listed in the calendar for Months One and Two at least six months before the event.

Many events can be pulled off with flair only a few months ahead of time. You may even put on an event Fast!—within a few weeks. Whether you plan to do a yearlong campaign, a mid-sized event, or a Fast! event, you must follow some basic steps. The following calendar contains the fundamental checkpoints on recruiting additional volunteers for almost any event, although the months may have to be condensed to fit your timetable.

Calendar Checklist for a Yearlong Campaign or Major Event

Month One

(Seven to ten months before major event)

❏ Form your committee.

❏ Design a Volunteer Task Form for use by committee chairs in requesting help.

❏ Design a Volunteer Availability Form that can be filled out by volunteers, by you, or by an assistant who is calling people to get them to volunteer.

❏ Update Status Report.

Month Two

(At least six months before major event)

❏ Set up a database to record tasks and availability as forms come in from chairs and volunteers.

❏ Update Status Report.

Month Three

(Five months before major event)

❏ Call members of the organization who are not yet on a committee or in the volunteer database and seek their services.

❏ Update Status Report.

Month Four

(Four months before major event)

❏ Work with your own contacts or with the Donations Chair to come up with small rewards for volunteers, especially those with onerous tasks.

❏ Update Status Report.

Month Five

(Three months before major event)

❏ Continue to seek the appropriate number of volunteers.

❏ Update Status Report.

Month Six

(Two months before the event)

❏ Assign volunteers to duties with other committees, such as phone solicitation.

❏ Update Status Report.

Month Seven

(One month before the event)

❏ Check with other committee chairs to determine their needs for volunteers the day of the event.

❏ Update Status Report.

One week before the event

☐ Make certain the volunteers know the seating charts, as well as the whereabouts of the restrooms, telephones, coatrooms, registration tables, private reception rooms, or other pertinent information for the guests.

☐ Make certain the volunteers know the dress code for the event.

☐ Assign volunteers to duties at the event, such as handing out programs or showing guests to their tables.

☐ Rehearse volunteers.

☐ Update Status Report.

Day of the event

☐ Arrive early to coordinate volunteers.

☐ Check to make certain volunteers are at their posts.

☐ Fill in where needed.

☐ Thank each volunteer during or after the event.

Month Eight

(Within two weeks after the event)

☐ Complete post-event written report for Event Chair.

☐ Hold event team wrap-up meeting, while details of the event are fresh.

Month Nine

(One month after the event)

❏ Take care of thank-you notes and calls.

❏ Critique the event.

Month Ten

(Two months after the event)

❏ Set up the calendar for a new project.

Forms and Outlines

Status Report

Duplicate this form for each of your subchair people and for yourself. Use it to monitor committee status monthly, periodically, or at each committee meeting. Have the chair list the committee's responsibilities for that period, who is in charge of each, the deadline, budget, and status at the time of each report. After the event, you will have a running time line for the next event team to use in planning. Here is a sample report. The blank one follows.

Status Report
(refer to monthly calendar)

Chair Person: Volunteers   Dick Coons
Event: MS Costume Ball
Current Date: April 10, 2000
Event Date: October 10, 2000

Item	Responsible Person	Due Date	Status	Budget
Form Committee	Dick Coons	4/30/00	All positions filled	-0-
Design a Volunteer Task Form for use by committee chairs in requesting help	Ellen Weisel	4/15/00	Designed and distributed to committees	
Design a Volunteer Availability Form	Ellen Weisel	5/1/00	Designed and ready for submissions	

Status Report
(refer to monthly calendar)

Chair Person: Volunteers
Event:
Current Date:
Event Date:

Item	Responsible Person	Due Date	Status	Budget

Volunteer Availability Form

Name	Address	Phone	E-mail	Availability

Cleanup Chair

Responsibilities

- Oversee the post-event cleanup.

Qualifications

- Good organizer.
- Experience in working with teams.

Planning the Cleanup

- Understand how much cleanup will be required, whether that means vacuuming up every piece of confetti, stacking the chairs, or just turning off the lights, securing the floor, and leaving it all for the janitor, caterer, or trash-removal company.
- Determine who will perform the cleanup chores that are the event's responsibility. Don't forget that once the event is concluded, workers are exhausted and may just

want to go home or go out for celebratory cocktails.
Make certain the cleanup committee workers know
their responsibilities and don't vanish into the night. If
the budget allows, consider hiring out the "dirty" parts
of the cleanup.

- Make certain the cleanup requirements of the location
  are known and met.

- Line up one or two workers with vans or recreational
  vehicles to haul materials you want retrieved. Arrange
  for a truck, if you must return larger items such as
  tables, chairs, or large decorations.

- Arrange through purchase, donation, or loan to have at
  the site all items you and your cleanup crew will need,
  if you are doing the "dirty" part of the cleanup.
  Depending on the event and location, items may include
  trash bags, bag ties, brooms, dustpans, mops, buckets,
  paper towels, spray cleaners, and so forth.

- If your event is outdoors during the day or early
  evening, make sure lighting will be available for cleanup
  that must be completed after dark.

Implementing the Cleanup

- Work with Arrangements and Logistics Chair to set up a
  "lost and found" where guests can call for left-behind
  scarves, purses, and other items. Retrieve such items
  and take them to the designated lost-and-found. Do not
  leave items at site. You may get a phone call from the
  frantic owners. You will create goodwill for next year, if
  you can send them the items. Phone the owner of any
  item that contains identification.

- Gather up all materials (such as computers, disks,
  audio/visual equipment, cell phones, extra gifts, leftover
  auction items, name tags, banners, pencils, lists, trays,

etc.) that you want to save. Take them with you following the event. Do not leave items at the site, if you ever want to see them again. Even trying to retrieve items from site officials the next day may be a major headache. Shifts change, and items become lost or misplaced.

- Make a final inspection, then shut off lights, lock the door, check with the registration desk, or do whatever final shutdown or check-out tasks are required.

- If cleanup items are borrowed, or if you are responsible for the return of items used during the event, keep a list or notebook specifying each item; its condition when borrowed; and the person, address, directions, phone number, and time-window applicable for its return. Make sure the person making the return contacts the person to whom the item is being returned, or leaves it in a secure place as agreed upon in advance. Get a return receipt for items returned to a commercial renting or leasing firm.

Calendar

Establishing Your Calendar

As Cleanup Chair, your duties will chiefly occur during the final month. Your calendar has been abbreviated to reflect this activity. It contains the fundamental checkpoints for almost any event.

Calendar Checklist for a Yearlong Campaign or Major Event

Months One-Six

(Two to ten months before event)

- ☐ Form Cleanup Committee of hardy, patient workers.
- ☐ Check with Arrangements Committee on cleanup needs for proposed site. Site may have in-house or an outside contracted cleanup crew that you are required to use.
- ☐ Update Status Report periodically as needed.

Month Seven

(One month before event)

- ☐ Form a "lost-and-found department."
- ☐ Double check with site management or Arrangements Chair to make certain all regulations are being met and ask about any last-minute changes.
- ☐ Determine the requirements for cleaning up the parking site. Red carpets may need to be rolled up and stored. Posters may have to be removed.

☐ Line up a truck or other vehicle or two for hauling away materials after event.

☐ Update Status Report.

One week before the event

☐ Check with Entertainment and Auction Chair for how that committee plans to wrap up its activities and how the Cleanup Committee will participate.

☐ Update Status Report.

Day of the event

☐ Have trash bags and other cleanup equipment available.

☐ Check with your cleanup crew by phone to make certain each person knows his or her duties and has no last-minute office or family chores that will prevent staying late.

☐ Check for audio/video or other equipment inadvertently left behind.

☐ Check for items lost by guests. If any, collect and take home or to your office, wherever the location of previously arranged "lost and found."

☐ Check parking lot for trash.

Month Eight

(Within two weeks after event)

☐ Complete post-event written report for Event Chair.

☐ Return all borrowed cleanup equipment.

☐ Return all lost-and-found items that have been claimed.

Months Nine-Ten

(One-two months after event)

❑ Take care of thank-you notes and calls.

❑ Submit suggestions for fine-tuning next year's event.

❑ Set up calendar for a new project.

❑ Donate to charity or dispose of unclaimed items from lost and found.

Forms and Outlines

Status Report

Duplicate this form for each of your subchair people and for yourself. Use it to monitor committee status monthly, periodically, or at each committee meeting. Have the chair list the committee's responsibilities for that period, who is in charge of each, the deadline, budget, and status at the time of each report. After the event, you will have a running time line for the next event team to use in planning. Here is a sample report. The blank one follows.

Status Report
(refer to monthly calendar)

Chair Person: Cleanup   Joe O'Connor
Event: MS Costume Ball
Current Date: April 10, 2000
Event Date: October 10, 2000

Item	Responsible Person	Due Date	Status	Budget
Form a "lost-and-found department"	Joe O'Connor	9/30/00	Arranged at coat check room	-0-
Double check with Arrangements Chair to make certain all regulations are being met and ask if there are any last-minute changes	Joe	10/1/00	No changes	
Establish the requirements for cleaning up the parking site	Joe	10/1/00	All red carpets must be returned to B&B Rental	
Line up a truck or other vehicle for hauling away materials after event	Bill Griffin	10/10/00	Browns have volunteered their pickup and van	

Status Report
(refer to monthly calendar)

Chair Person: Cleanup
Event:
Current Date:
Event Date:

Item	Responsible Person	Due Date	Status	Budget

Index